Canadian Policy Research Networks Inc. (CPRN)
600 – 250 Albert Street, Ottawa, Ontario K1P 6M1
Tel: (613) 567-7500   Fax: (613) 567-7640
Web Site: www.cprn.org

Without a Roadmap: Government Funding and Regulation of Canada's Universities and Colleges

Ken Snowdon
Snowdon & Associates Inc.

The opinions expressed herein are those of the author,
and do not necessarily reflect the opinions of the funding organizations.

© 2005 Canadian Policy Research Networks Inc.

Table of Contents

Foreword i
Author's Preface iii
Executive Summary v
Acknowledgements ix

1. Introduction 1
2. Setting the Context 3
3. **Funding Trends – Early 1990s to the Present** 6
   3.1. Post-secondary Financial and Enrolment Data – Considerations 6
   3.2. Total Funding to Universities and Colleges 6
   3.3. PSE Funding: Recognizing Restrictions on Certain Sources of Income ... 8
   3.4. PSE Funding: Shifts in Income 10
   3.5. PSE Income: Changes in Income 11
      a. *Total Government Expenditures on Higher Education* 13
      b. *Provincial Funding* 14
      c. *Federal Funding* 17
      d. *Other Sources of Revenue* 18
      e. *Institutional Impacts* 19
4. **Funding Comparisons** 21
5. **Funding Mechanisms** 24
   5.1. Characteristics of Funding Mechanisms in Canada 24
   5.2. Provincial Funding Mechanisms 26
   5.3. Federal Funding Mechanisms 31
      a. *Federal Research Initiatives* 31
      b. *Federal Initiatives on Student Aid* 34
6. **The Regulatory Environment: Tuition, Degree-granting and Accountability** 36
   6.1. Tuition 36
   6.2. Developments in Degree-granting 38
   6.3. Accountability 39
   6.4. Changes in Funding Mechanisms and the Regulatory Environment: Impact on Internal Resource Allocation 42
7. **Access: What Do We Know?** 45
8. **Quality: What Do We Know?** 50

9. Assessment of Funding Levels and Incentive Structures	56
10. Conclusions: Key Considerations in Improving Quality and Access	60
10.1. Concluding Comments	64
Appendix A: Funding and Enrolment	65
Appendix B: Summary of Provincial Allocation Mechanisms and Regulatory Developments	73
References	79
Our Support	87

Foreword

Universities and colleges have experienced a radical shift in circumstances in the past 20 years. The demand for advanced education has soared as the skill requirements for a good job escalated. Yet, until recently, governments have been cutting transfers to cover operations. This revenue has been replaced in part by higher tuition fees and more active fundraising programs. But there have also been notable changes in the way university programs are organized such as the increase in class size and greater use of part-time lecturers and sessional teachers. Nevertheless, educational attainment of the Canadian population has risen as young people and mature workers have expanded their participation in higher education.

Canadians are vitally aware of the importance of advanced education. They know that Canada's competitiveness and their own future living standards will depend on the knowledge and skills of the work force. The main worry, as tuition costs increased, has been whether all qualified students have been able to access the appropriate university or college program. Both governments and philanthropists have therefore made significant investments in student aid through loans, grants, and bursaries. And CPRN has contributed several major papers examining their success in ensuring access(available at www.cprn.org).

So far, however, few questions have been asked about trends in the quality of the learning experience of students. Are Canada's universities and colleges able to match the quality of teaching and research provided by the best schools in other countries? What policy changes might be needed to allow our post-secondary institutions to realize their potential for excellence without compromising access?

With the help of funding from the Wilson Foundation, CPRN has launched a series of studies of quality issues in our post-secondary system. Our goal is to launch a national conversation about this issue. This report, by Ken Snowdon, looks at the incentive structure (funding and regulation) facing post-secondary institutions in Canada. It documents the difficulties that our universities and colleges have had in coping with changing, and sometimes conflicting, government policies over the past 15 years. Funding per student is below what it was in 1992-93 in six provinces. Add to that the range of cost pressures on the system: growing research mandates, technological change, growing need for student support services, and a mounting deficit in building maintenance, and the pressures on quality are self-evident.

Unfortunately, our ability to document the impact on quality is limited, as Ross Finnie and Alex Usher documented in the first report in this series: *Measuring the Quality of Post-secondary Education: Concepts, Current Practices and a Strategic Plan.* They provided a broad conceptual framework for thinking about the quality of the learning experience, and identified strategies for building a Canadian measurement system. This report by Ken Snowdon identifies the need for a new policy context: with greater clarity about goals, multi-year funding arrangements, accountability frameworks focused on results, recognition of institutional differentiation and better information to inform policy development. Snowdon also points to a crying need to improve 'trust' among the PSE partners.

The next paper in the series will examine cases studies of innovation and differentiation in our universities and colleges. A fourth and final paper will synthesize the key findings and explore the policy implications.

I would like to thank Ken Snowdon for his pan-Canadian perspective on the challenges that our post-secondary institutions have faced, and for setting out principles that should characterize federal and provincial policies to fund and regulate our colleges and universities in the future. I would also like to thank The Wilson Foundation, and the Ontario Ministry of Training, Colleges and Universities for their financial support for this study. A complete list of funders for the series on quality issues in Canada's post-secondary institutions can be found under "Our Support" at the end of this report.

Judith Maxwell
December 2005

Author's Preface

From the outset this paper was intended to draw on existing reports and analyses to examine the impact of funding mechanisms and the regulatory environment on access and quality in Canadian post-secondary education. The fact is, however, that little has been written about funding *mechanisms* in the post-secondary sector. Moreover, because of the major differences in the structure and operation of provincial higher education systems across the country it has only been possible to 'scratch the surface' of the murky depths of college and university funding and provincial funding mechanisms. How public funds are <u>*allocated*</u> is (almost) as important as how <u>*much*</u> funding is allocated. And, to what end? Government announcements tend to focus on the latter point and highlight the intended use of the funds – improve access, improve quality, improve performance, increase enrolment, finance new facilities. Little is said about how the funds find their way to the institutions to actually 'get the job done' or how those monies relate to other resources such as tuition, private giving or research contracts, or how government policy and regulations ("the rules of the game") affect the distribution and utilization of those funds. This paper provides a glimpse into the latter realities, but it is only a glimpse.

To better understand the import of funding mechanisms, and the impact of changes in funding mechanisms, it is important to understand a bit about the intricacies and complexities of post-secondary funding – an ultimately enlightening topic for those who can withstand the soporific details of 'fund-accounting'. Accordingly, part of this paper provides some necessary background to understanding the various pieces of the post-secondary funding puzzle.

In the case of the regulatory environment more research is available, especially as it relates to the topics of tuition policy, degree-granting authority and accountability. Nevertheless, nowhere is the phrase 'the devil is in the details' more apt than when exploring the intricacies of provincial policies and regulations in the post-secondary sphere (with the possible exception, of course, of examining government funding *mechanisms*). Again, this paper only 'scratches the surface' of a complex web of provincially focused policies and regulations that govern post-secondary education in this country.

The paper has some major limitations. It 'tilts' towards the university sector and some provinces are highlighted more than others, due largely, in both cases, to the availability of research material but also to time and space constraints. Further, it ignores important regulatory issues relating to international students and the mobility of Canadian students. However, to the extent that this paper sparks others to conduct further research, those acknowledged shortcomings will be addressed in the future.

December, 2005

Executive Summary

This report focuses on government *funding mechanisms* and the post-secondary *regulatory environment* and their impact on the ability of post-secondary institutions to meet access demands and provide a quality learning experience. The main contention of this report is straightforward: the story of higher education in Canada since the early 1990s is heavily influenced by three key factors: federal funding, changing demographics, and the adoption of what has been described as "a climate of neo-liberal market-based philosophy." Throw in a little Y2K hysteria, the implosion of the dot.com revolution and the fall-out from 9/11 and you have an environment characterized by major upheavals, significant change and constant fiscal pressures.

Each province dealt with the preceding factors differently depending on its own particular circumstances, and provincial circumstances differ in many ways – from the structure of the post-secondary system to the realities of the post-secondary demographic, and from the philosophy about 'who should pay' to the stance on expanding degree-granting privileges. Funding and regulatory developments at the provincial and federal levels combined to create a period of unprecedented change (and uncertainty) in the post-secondary landscape. That, in turn, created an environment where colleges and universities were constantly reacting to government actions which, too often, were ill-considered, suffered from less than stellar implementation, and placed undue stresses on the post-secondary sector.

Key findings from this report:

- From a funding perspective the period is marked by two distinct periods – retrenchment from the early 1990s to the latter 1990s – and reinvestment from that point onwards;
- total funding to colleges and universities, from all sources and for all purposes, reached an all-time high of an estimated $27.7 billion in 2004-05, an increase of over $11 billion since the early 1990s;
- once inflation and reporting changes are taken into account, the "real" increase falls to about $6 billion or approximately 30percent;
- once increased enrolment is taken into account, per student funding for colleges and universities in 6 of 10 provinces is below 1992-93 levels;
- an expanded research mandate has resulted in additional cost pressures that further erode the per student level of funding;
- because of restrictions on the use of some of the monies, the actual increase for *core operating* requirements is lessened further;
- there have been significant shifts in funding sources over time with considerably greater emphasis on tuition, more emphasis on private funding (i.e., donations, private contracts) and considerably less emphasis on provincial grants;
- federal research funding, and research funding in general, increased markedly since the latter part of the 1990s; and
- revenue diversification resulted in some unexpected consequences for institutions and governments.

Against that funding background:

- allocation mechanisms at both the provincial and federal levels have generally become more complicated and are being used to 'steer' results;
- the regulatory environment has become increasingly complicated, especially in areas where government has attempted to introduce more competition and market principles;
- heightened interest in accountability led to increased audit requirements and additional reporting with an emphasis on compliance rather than outcomes
- in some cases federal and provincial funding is, in fact, 'working at cross-purposes';
- access increased – though there is room for improvement and much of the increase is the direct result of more recent government funding initiatives that recognize the importance of increasing capacity;
- concerns about 'quality' are beginning to resonate with provincial governments even though there are many different views of 'quality'; and
- provincial differences in the demography of the post-secondary age cohort have had, and will continue to have, a major impact on provincial funding commitments.

Key considerations in improving access and quality.

What are you trying to do? (goals, objectives)
- In consultation and partnership with the institutions that have the responsibility for making it happen, government must articulate the access and quality goals. Those goals will be, and should be, defined differently by province and by institution.
- Steps must be taken to improve the climate of trust among all of the partners with an interest in delivering high quality post-secondary education: federal government, provincial governments, colleges and universities.

What do you need to get there? (strategies, tools, resources)
- Adequate resources must be available – from somewhere. It is government's responsibility to be clear about its funding commitment and clear about the expectations for the funding commitment.
- Recognize that improving access for under-represented groups will require higher than average levels of resources for support services.
- Adopt a multi-year perspective. For much of the past fifteen years colleges and universities have been operating on a year-to-year basis in an environment where funding announcements are late, where changes in funding mechanisms have been made with little consultation, and where the lack of predictability has negatively affected institutional planning; an environment that is far from optimal to address access and quality concerns.
- Keep the funding mechanism(s) few and simple. It is imperative that governments and the post-secondary institutions fully understand the consequences of funding changes and changes in funding mechanisms. The more complicated the funding mechanisms and the more mechanisms there are, the more likely the full consequences will not be appreciated, nor understood.
- Create a climate where private giving and institutional entrepreneurial activity is clearly seen as providing the 'margin of excellence' and a funding source for differentiation and

diversification, rather than as a substitute for government funds or as a source of funds for the province or federal government to leverage.

How would you know that you are making progress? (indicators, public reporting, accountability)
- Adopt an accountability framework that recognizes the complexities of post-secondary institutions and the multiplicity of goals associated with a college or university.
- Emphasize performance reporting with each institution defining access and quality in terms of its own circumstances, mission and particular strengths.
- Rely on the involvement of post-secondary governance bodies to monitor and report on progress towards goals.

Other Considerations:

- The federal/provincial 'overlap' in the post-secondary sector is not conducive to optimizing investments in access and quality. Steps must be taken to delineate the respective roles.
- Good, consistent, reliable, up-to-date information is a prerequisite to making informed decisions. Efforts must be made to improve the timeliness, quality and breadth of post-secondary information (e.g., enrolment, staffing, financial information) published by provincial and federal governments.
- Further research in the following areas would improve understanding of the many factors that influence access and quality:
  - the need for better comparative financial and enrolment information with other countries;
  - the need for more comparative information about funding *mechanisms* in other countries;
  - the need to catalogue, chronicle and assess the evolving approaches to accountability;
  - the link between quality assurance and quality improvement;
  - the development of output and outcome quality measures;
  - the 'opening up' of the post-secondary system and the impact on competition;
  - an evaluation of rankings and licensure requirements, program reviews and various indicators of satisfaction; and
  - an examination of the impact of the major increase in research funding on research quality and graduate education.

This paper provides a glimpse of how funding mechanisms and the regulatory environment can affect the ability of post-secondary institutions to address access and quality concerns. There has been a marked change in government attitudes towards post-secondary education over the past few years, in particular, and improving access and quality are now twin goals that seem to be found in report after report across the country. Moreover, it is now apparent that governments are prepared to 're-invest' in post-secondary education and improve capacity. In that regard, the lessons of the past offer a guide for the future.

Acknowledgements

The author gratefully acknowledges the support and assistance of a number of individuals whose ideas, help with data and willingness to discuss various aspects of the project and comments on early drafts are deeply appreciated: Herb O'Heron for his encyclopaedic memory of post-secondary information and his insightful comments and unfailing good humour; Alex Usher for opening my eyes to the international dimensions of the quality debate; Glen Jones for pointing me towards the AIHEPS[1] initiative; and two anonymous reviewers for focused comments that led to major rewrites and expansions of specific sections.

To Judith Maxwell, Ron Saunders and the CPRN project management team, thank you for your support throughout the project, and to Ron, additional thanks for the thoughtful comments on early drafts.

---

[1] The Alliance for International Higher Education Policy Studies (AIHEPS) http://www.nyu.edu/iesp/aiheps/ , has been established to " improve comparative understanding of how changes in higher education policies (rules of the game) alter the nature of institutional behaviors and system performance." Canadian researchers are engaged in that project and their efforts – with a focus on British Columbia, Ontario and Quebec - will, no doubt, cast considerably more light on these issues in the future.

x

1. Introduction

The provincial and federal governments play major roles in the post-secondary arena and in the provision of higher education opportunities. *Access* has long been the primary consideration of both levels of government with post-secondary education seen as a key instrument of social mobility. More recently, the economic virtue of post-secondary investment has re-emerged as a major rationale for public investment, often in the context of strengthening competitiveness in a global economy; *quality* post-secondary education is part of the competitiveness equation.

This report focuses on government *funding mechanisms* and the post-secondary *regulatory environment* to determine the impact of those two factors on the ability of post-secondary institutions to meet access demands and provide a quality learning experience. The report reviews core funding mechanisms in the college and university sector(s) in each of the provinces and at the federal level. The regulatory environment review focuses on the provinces and changes in three key policy areas that have an impact on the post-secondary sector: tuition policy; degree granting authorization; and accountability requirements. Due to the availability of source material, greater emphasis is placed on the university sector and developments in particular provinces.

Federal initiatives such as the Canada Foundation for Innovation (CFI), Canada Research Chairs (CRC), allowance for indirect costs of research, and the various federal scholarship/student assistance programs are addressed as well. To set the context for the discussion about funding mechanisms and the regulatory environment, funding trends for colleges and universities since the early 1990s are examined along with funding developments and trends in the Unites States and the United Kingdom.

The main contention of this report is straightforward: the story of higher education in Canada over the past fifteen years is heavily influenced by three key factors: federal funding, changing demographics, and the adoption of what has been described as "a climate of neo-liberal market-based philosophy."[2] Throw in a little Y2K hysteria, the implosion of the dot.com revolution and the fall-out from 9/11 and you have an environment characterized by major upheavals, significant change and constant fiscal pressures.

Each province dealt with the preceding key factors differently depending on their own particular circumstances. Funding and regulatory developments at the provincial and federal levels combined to create a period of unprecedented change (and uncertainty) in the post-secondary landscape. That, in turn, created an environment where colleges and universities were constantly reacting to government actions which, too often, were ill-considered, suffered from less than stellar implementation, and placed undue stresses on the post-secondary sector.

The results are mixed: access improved, especially in more recent years, but less so than it might have under other circumstances; quality, if one focuses solely on the student learning environment, appears to have decreased. Universities and colleges are different places now than they were in 1990. Pulled and pushed by government actions that led to major shifts in the

---

[2] Dennison, J.D., and Schuetze, H.G., *Extending Access, Choice and the Reign of the Market*, The Canadian Journal of Higher Education, Volume XXXIV-3, 2004 p.19

sources of funding, more government regulation and intervention, and added expectations, the post-secondary sector in many provinces is struggling to reconcile the increasingly complex roles of social and economic catalyst with increased research expectations and burgeoning student demand.

The report that follows explores the previous themes in more detail. After a 'setting the context' overview, the report provides a review of funding trends and the factors affecting funding trends. That section is followed by a brief review of funding comparisons with other countries. The report then turns to an examination of funding mechanisms and regulatory mechanisms, the latter focusing on tuition, degree granting and accountability. What we know about access and quality are the focus of sections 7 and 8. The penultimate section merges the analysis of funding and regulatory mechanisms with the findings regarding access and quality and provides an interpretation of the impact. A final section then provides a summary of considerations that may help foster an environment that is conducive to improving quality and access. Two appendices provide more detailed information about funding levels, and funding and regulatory mechanisms.

2. Setting the Context

Canada's post-secondary landscape differs markedly from province to province reflecting history, local circumstances and different approaches to the provision of post-secondary opportunities.[3] Those differences shape the post-secondary sector and post-secondary institutions in a multitude of ways, from mission to program 'mix', admission policy to graduation rates, and from governance to government relations. Commenting on a series of essays outlining post-secondary arrangements across Canada, Michael Skolnik, an authority on such matters, observed that:

> Overall, perhaps the most striking conclusion ... is the great diversity of situations surrounding higher education across the country. Beneath the surface of apparent binary structures or as provinces move away from the straightforward binary structures, the essays reveal substantial differences with respect to composition, vision, and direction for their higher education systems.[4]

To further lend credence to the notion of interprovincial differences, if one focuses only on a single topic – degree accreditation – it has been noted that:

> ... each province has developed unique procedures with regard to the approval of new institutions and credentials. There are interprovincial differences regarding the recognition of non-public institutions or credentials, the right of institutions to grant different credentials, and the relationship between the various types.[5]

Against a landscape of provincial differences, the federal government operates a set of post-secondary programs (research, training, student assistance) that cut across provincial boundaries. Those programs engender local responses that range from full embrace to outright rejection, once again reflecting history, local circumstances and the constant tension of federal/provincial relations. Provinces react differently to the federal presence and the impact on funding arrangements for higher education can differ, significantly, as a result.

Since 1990 major changes have occurred in the post-secondary sector across the country. In the face of an economic slow-down in the early 1990s and impending cut-backs in federal transfers, provincial governments launched reviews and appointed commissions to help grapple with the realities of public finance. A period of relatively stable enrolment in the mid-1990s gave way to major increases in post-secondary demand fuelled by, what David Foot coined, the "baby-boom echo"[6] and increasing awareness of the importance of obtaining a post-secondary qualification, leading to rising rates of participation in PSE. This, in turn, gave rise to another round of reviews and commissions. From a funding perspective the period is marked by two distinct periods – retrenchment from the early 1990s to the latter 1990s – and then reinvestment from that point onwards. In both cases, the federal government played a major role.

---

[3] G.A. Jones, *Higher Education in Canada: Different systems, different perspectives*, Garland Publishing, 1997.
[4] M. Skolnik, *Putting it Altogether: Viewing Canadian Higher Education from a Collection of Jurisdiction-Based Perspectives*, in Ibid., p. 341
[5] D. Marshall, *Degree Accreditation in Canada*, The Canadian Journal of Higher Education, Volume XXXIV, No.2, 2004 p.73.
[6] D.K Foot, *Boom Bust Echo 2000*, Macfarlane, Walter & Ross, Toronto, 1996, p.30

After cutting transfer payments to the provinces in the mid-90s and seemingly backing away from increased responsibilities in the higher education sector, the federal government re-asserted and re-inserted itself through a series of new initiatives aimed at improving research capacity and student access.[7] In the process, new acronyms were added to the post-secondary lexicon with the introduction of the Canada Foundation for Innovation (CFI), Canada Research Chairs (CRC) and Canada Millennium Scholarship Foundation (CMSF). The renewed presence of the federal government at a time when the post-secondary sector was coping with straitened circumstances, placed much greater emphasis on research and added a major dynamic to the post-secondary environment.

The regulatory environment experienced significant changes as well. In the face of fiscal constraints at the provincial level, new directions in public finance became imperative. Existing government funding allocation mechanisms were reviewed and altered. Tuition 'policy' embarked on a roller-coaster ride in many provinces and, in some instances, resulted in a multi-faceted regulatory framework known more for its complexity than its coherence. Many provinces made major changes to their student aid programs, moving from largely grant-based systems to largely loan-based systems, and placing greater funding and administrative responsibility on the institutions. Later in the decade, in response to the reality of the 'baby-boom echo', some provinces opened their systems to the private sector and expanded the degree granting roles of colleges. Quality assurance became a watchword. And, under the banner of accountability, governments introduced a host of reporting requirements and accountability frameworks that continue to evolve.

The funding and regulatory environments were also greatly affected by what has been referred to as the neo-liberal market-based philosophy – characterized by a reliance on the 'market', reductions in the size of government, tax reductions, government deregulation, privatization of government services/assets, greater emphasis on individual responsibility and more emphasis on private benefits than the public good.[8] For much of the period in question various governments adopted all or parts of the 'philosophy' and, through various instruments, attempted to implement the philosophy in a variety of public policy fields, including higher education. The implications of government action are still being felt; attempts to rely on the market were often quickly replaced with greater government controls (i.e., tuition), efforts to deregulate and eliminate 'red-tape' in some sectors were replaced with more regulation and 'red-tape' in other sectors – often under the banner of accountability. Attempts to move to greater individual responsibility translated into more student debt, a need to revamp programs and regulations to address student debt loads, and a student assistance environment that is referred to as a "hodge podge of programs" and characterized as "dauntingly complex".[9] The point is a general change in philosophy led to an extended period of experimentation, in a host of post-secondary policy

---

[7] David Cameron argues that, in fact, the federal interest in research was actually launched during the Mulroney years but 'put on hold' until the federal fiscal situation improved sufficiently to begin major investments. (See D. Cameron, in Taking Public Universities Seriously pp.280-81)

[8] There are various definitions associated with the term neo-liberalism. The characterization is not intended to be comprehensive but, rather, to capture the main elements.

[9] Finnie, R., et al, "Meeting the Need: A New Architecture for Canada's Student Financial Aid System", in Beach, C.M., et.al., *Higher Education in Canada*, p.496-497

areas, that simply added more complexity (and in some instances, chaos) to the higher education environment, along with, ironically, considerably more government intervention.[10]

The post-secondary sector was also affected by other factors that had a significant impact on the latter part of the 1990s and early part of the new century. Many institutions had to make significant investments in information systems to address the concerns of 'Y2K'. Those investments in time, money, people, and process change were non-trivial and plagued many institutions throughout the latter part of the 1990s (and after) in the run-up to the year 2000. The dot.com 'boom' fuelled interest in targeted enrolment expansion in programs such as computer science, electrical engineering and, ultimately, almost any program with the word "technology" in it. Colleges and universities responded to expansion incentives and created a mini-boom in the scramble for faculty in selected disciplines and for investment in new technology. The new wealth generated by the buoyant investment scene became the ready source of 'matching' funding for capital expansion and other fund-raising priorities. The dot.com 'bust' had multiple negative impacts that are still being felt. Finally, the tragedy of 9/11 and its aftermath created its own set of challenges for the post-secondary sector, from security concerns and international student and faculty recruitment issues to the impact on investment markets and the economy.

Looking back, the one truism that seems applicable is "May you live in interesting times".

---

[10] In *The Use of Market Mechanisms in Higher Education Finance and State Control*, Young argues that the 'marketization' of higher education actually "adds yet another instrument to the state's formidable tool box that assists in regulating and controlling higher education." p. 82 in The Canadian Journal of Higher Education, Vol. XXXII, No.2, 2002

3. Funding Trends – early 1990s to the present

3.1. Post-secondary Financial and Enrolment Data – Considerations

Attempting to provide definitive statements about higher education funding levels nationally and provincially is complicated by a number of factors. As noted previously Canada's higher education landscape is actually more akin to a patchwork of provincial frameworks that differ in scale, emphasis, tradition, history and many other elements. While attempts are made to establish national reporting standards, in fact there are significant differences in the reporting practices of colleges and universities across the country and within provincial boundaries.[11] Changes in reporting practices have been a constant reality over the past fifteen years, simply adding to the difficulty in attempting to develop reliable, consistent, comparable financial statistics. When one adds the fact that there is no agreed to national definition of a 'student' it makes more detailed comparisons of funding on a per student basis even more difficult. Moreover, the lack of consistent, reliable up-to-date enrolment information is a serious deficiency. While there are Statistics Canada financial reports that provide an overview of university and college finance, there are data limitations that directly impact temporal and interprovincial comparisons. Nevertheless, to establish some general trends in post-secondary funding, we begin with an aggregate view of post-secondary financing.

3.2. Total Funding to Universities and Colleges

Total funding for post-secondary education has never been higher in absolute terms. For 2004-05, Statistics Canada estimates that total funding for colleges and universities was about $27.7 billion and has increased by over $11 billion since 1992-93.[12] General inflation (CPI) over that period knocks about $4 billion off the purchasing power of that increase, and changes in reporting knock off another billion, but, regardless, the number appears impressive and translates into an inflation adjusted percentage increase of about 30% (see Appendix A). In the same period, however, several factors have affected the 'purchasing power' of that increase: significant enrolment increases, a major expansion in research activity and a host of cost pressures that exceed CPI.

Since the early 1990s, enrolment has increased markedly. While up-to-date enrolment information is not available from Statistics Canada beyond 2003 for universities and 1999 for colleges, reasonable estimates indicate that university full-time enrolment increased well beyond 40percent [13] with much of the increase occurring since the latter part of the 1990s, and full-time college enrolment increased by an estimated 35 percent. Appendix A provides funding and enrolment information by province that indicates total funding per student, from all sources and for <u>all purposes</u>, is less now (2004-05) than in 1992-93, after adjusting for enrolment and inflation (CPI), in six of ten provinces as illustrated in Figure 1. If one could adjust the data for changes in reporting over the period, the per student funding levels would be lower still.

---

[11] See the author's *Muddy Data: University Financing in Canada*, in Higher Education in Canada, for a more detailed review of some of the factors that affect comparisons of university financial data.
[12] Statistics Canada, Universities and colleges revenue and expenditures, CANSIM 385-0007
[13] *Price of Knowledge, 2004* Figures 2.II.10 and 2.II.3 and authors estimates from various reports.

Figure 1: Indexed Change in <u>TOTAL</u> Funding per Full-time Student
(All funds, all sources of income, adjusted for inflation) 1992=100

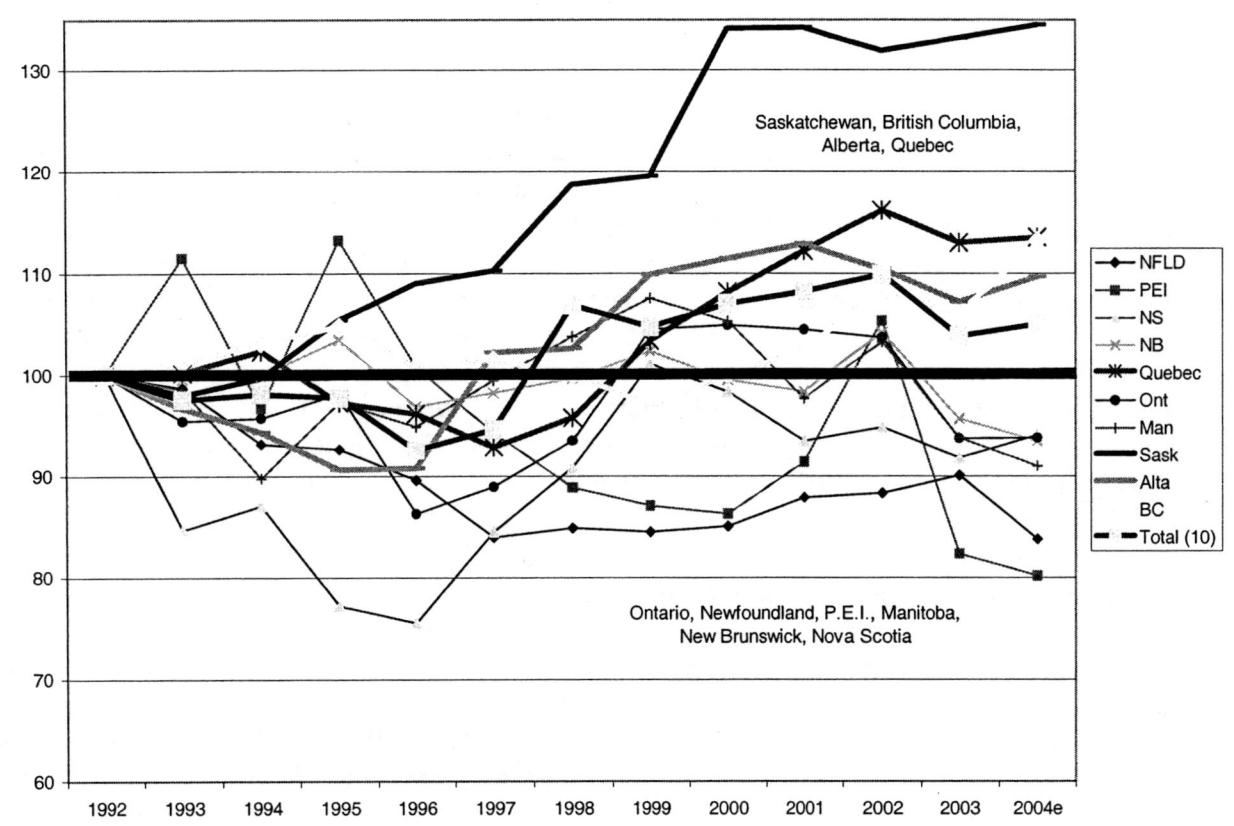

Source: See Appendix A

Using real increases in research funding as a proxy for research activity, the estimated increase in the university sector alone over the period has exceeded 170 percent![14] Together, the increases in research 'activity 'and enrolment help put the overall funding increase into perspective. A 30 percent increase in real funding does not cover the direct and indirect costs of increased enrolment and research. There are as well, a number of other factors that affect the interpretation of what, on the surface, looks like (and is) a significant increase in the absolute revenues available to post-secondary institutions.

Cost pressures are a reality for all parts of the post-secondary sector. People costs – salaries and benefits – are by far the largest proportion of **total** costs (approximately 55 percent) and there have been competitive pressures[15] to provide annual increases in excess of CPI, especially during the 'expansionary' period since the latter part of the 1990s. In terms of benefit costs, a host of regulatory changes and increases has contributed to an escalation in costs far beyond 'normal'

---

[14] There is some over reporting in this figure because of changes in reporting over the time period in question.
[15] Salary restraint in the early to mid-90s led to increased concern by the latter part of the decade about the ability of Canadian institutions to recruit faculty relative to the United States and the private sector. At a time when various scenarios projected a need for thousands of new faculty and, at a time when, 'brain drain' was in the news, the combination resulted in increased salary demands.

CPI.[16] At the same time, because of an aging workforce and other factors, utilization rates of insured benefits (e.g., supplementary medical coverage) have increased thus adding yet another pressure point.

A host of expenditure items comprise the other 45 percent of expenditures including library acquisitions, utilities, equipment, supplies, laboratory materials and chemicals. While there are examples of 'deflation' in some items such as desk-top computers there are many examples of inflationary cost pressures far exceeding CPI increases. According to a Price Index constructed by the Council of Ontario Universities, based on price indices from various sectors, major increases have occurred in such areas as library acquisitions.[17] More recently, readers will be familiar with the run-up in utilities costs. The point is not to dwell on particular cost items but simply to illustrate that there are significant cost pressures in the post-secondary sector and those pressures help put what look like major increases in post-secondary funding, in perspective. In the recent Ontario Post-secondary Review, the Honourable Bob Rae explicitly noted the importance of recognizing the "reality of price inflation." To ignore inflation in his proposed plan for re-investment would "put the achievement of access and quality goals in jeopardy."[18]

There are other cost pressures that have little to do with inflation but reflect other realities. For example, while the cost of desk-top computers and peripherals has decreased over time, the demand for information technology services has expanded considerably. Desk-top computers require infrastructure – networks, databases, and support services where the demand continues to grow at a rapid pace. Many institutions, for a variety of reasons ranging from preparation for Y2K, to improving business processes and compliance with government regulations, have invested heavily in administrative information technology systems. Another example is the cost associated with maintaining an expanding and aging physical plant. National estimates of deferred maintenance in the university sector alone totalled $3.6 billion in 2001.[19]

3.3. PSE Funding: Recognizing Restrictions on Certain Sources of Income

There is another major point to be made about the figure of $27.7 billion cited previously: it includes funding for everything – capital, research, ancillary operations and core operations – and includes revenue from all sources.

So what, one might say, a dollar is a dollar regardless of origin or purpose. In the post-secondary sector, however, where a dollar comes from often affects its purpose because of restrictions imposed by the 'funder'. The structure of post-secondary financing is a bit more complicated than simply looking at aggregate figures and hence deserves a closer look.

To better understand some of the complexities, and the impact on aggregate financial information, the following section deals exclusively with university financing because of the availability of more disaggregated financial statistics. Universities receive funding from a number of sources – governments, private donors, students, corporations, investments and the

---

[16] Council of Ontario Universities, *Resource Document 2004*, Table 8.3
[17] Ibid., Appendix D.
[18] Hon. Bob Rae, *Ontario: A Leader in Learning*, p.95
[19] Association of Universities and Colleges of Canada, *Trends in Higher Education*, p.72.

provision of services. Sometimes those monies are restricted for specific purposes. For example, an alumnus may donate money to support a scholarship. The university is acting as a steward of the donation, carrying out the wishes of the donor. Those monies are clearly "restricted" and only available for a specific purpose – as designated by the donor. Those funds, while they increase the overall level of university funding, are not available to pay salaries, to pay utility bills, to pay for library journals or maintain buildings. The same principle applies to other monies that universities receive. Provincial grants for capital purposes are to be used for new construction and renovations and repairs and there are strict reporting requirements. Government contracts and private research contracts are provided for a specific purpose with clear deliverables and specific reporting requirements. Research grants from the federal granting agencies (NSERC, CIHR and SSHRC) are similar in that the funds are provided for a specific purpose and there are separate accountability requirements. Universities (and colleges) also operate 'ancillary services' such as bookstores, residences, food services and parking services. As enrolments increase and the cost of services increase, the actual revenue may increase as well. Since many of the 'customers' for those services are students, faculty and staff, there tends to be significant customer input on service levels, quality levels and price. Over the past fifteen years many institutions have adopted financial policies that ensure all costs (direct and indirect) are recovered from the ancillary operations and appropriate reserves have been established for regular maintenance and refurbishment. In some cases those ancillary services generate 'profit' to help support educational purposes.

To recognize the restrictions associated with different sources of funding, the university sector adheres to what is called "fund accounting" whereby monies are classified for

> accounting and reporting purposes in accordance with activities or objectives as specified by donors, in accordance with regulations, restrictions, or limitations imposed by sources outside the institution, or in accordance with directions issued by the governing body of the institution.[20]

So, a university can be in receipt of additional revenues in certain FUNDS for specific purposes, but there may not be adequate increases in revenue to cover 'core operations' – salaries of faculty and staff, heat, light and water, library acquisitions, information technology, student services and the host of 'operating' expenditures that support the work of the institution.[21]

Universities (and colleges) do receive funds that are intended to be used to support 'core operations'. Those funds – primarily provincial operating grants and tuition – are intended to support general educational operations and often are the focus of the annual operating budget. Over the past fifteen years those monies have been the subject of more 'earmarking' thus reducing an institution's truly discretionary funding. Governments, in some provinces, for example, have legislated requirements that a portion of tuition increases must be set-aside for student assistance. Moreover, in many provinces, it is the core operating grants that have, in fact, been the subject of cut-backs, freezes or severely limited increases. If the provincial government

---

[20] Canadian Association of University Business Officers, *Financial Information of Universities and Colleges, Guidelines*, (2000-01) p.4

[21] Institutions will also place restrictions on some funds to create reserves – often in anticipation of major expenditures that are cyclical in nature (e.g., major information technology infrastructure, major capital maintenance projects).

chooses to provide additional funding it is often in the form of earmarked funding for specific purposes such as increasing enrolment in specified areas, or performance-based funding.

3.4. PSE Funding: Shifts in Income

The period since 1990 has seen a significant shift in both TYPE of income as well as the restricted purposes for that income as illustrated in Table 1 - based on the most recent financial statistics from the university sector in Canada. There are a number of interesting points about Table 1. First, in terms of income TYPE, one can see that tuition and other fees has doubled from about 11 percent of **total** income to 22 percent. Provincial grants and contracts have decreased from about 60 percent of total income to slightly above 40 percent, a decline of almost one-third. Federal grants have increased from 9 percent of total income to 11 percent while the other TYPEs of income have shown modest increases in the proportion of total. By FUND, the Operating Fund decreased from 66 percent to 61 percent[22] while the Research Fund increased from 14 percent of total income to 21 percent, with the remaining FUNDS essentially maintaining their share of overall income.

Table 1: Income by Type and Fund FY1990 and FY2004 ($000)

1989-90 FY90 Income by TYPE	Operating	Trust	Research	Ancillary	Capital	Total	Distribution by TYPE
Tuition & Other Fees	$ 993,331	$ 5,134	$ -	$ -	$ -	$ 998,465	11%
Provincial Grants and Contracts	$ 4,693,881	$ 78,797	$ 283,492	$ 5,167	$ 312,978	$ 5,374,315	61%
Federal Grants and Contracts	$ 16,234	$ 70,631	$ 671,584	$ 1,313	$ 5,689	$ 765,451	9%
Donations & Non-Gov't Grants/Contracts	$ 22,406	$ 190,409	$ 294,004	$ 947	$ 57,438	$ 565,204	6%
Investment Income	$ 96,351	$ 141,323	$ 13,649	$ 3,440	$ 29,018	$ 283,781	3%
Other Income & Sales of Service	$ 60,397	$ 22,367	$ 11,119	$ 754,390	$ 43,751	$ 892,024	10%
Total Incnome	$ 5,882,600	$ 508,661	$ 1,273,848	$ 765,257	$ 448,874	$ 8,879,240	100%
Distribution by FUND	66%	6%	14%	9%	5%	100%	

2003-04 FY04 Income by TYPE	Operating	Trust	Research	Ancillary	Capital	Total	Distribution by TYPE
Tuition & Other Fees	$ 4,217,566	$ 64,347	$ -	$ -	$ -	$ 4,281,913	22%
Provincial Grants and Contracts	$ 6,773,250	$ 201,516	$ 995,016	$ 7,544	$ 606,643	$ 8,583,969	43%
Federal Grants and Contracts	$ 69,546	$ 61,672	$ 2,110,048	$ 42	$ 19,346	$ 2,260,654	11%
Donations & Non-Gov't Grants/Contracts	$ 88,661	$ 384,389	$ 830,365	$ 6,907	$ 140,947	$ 1,451,269	7%
Investment Income	$ 241,871	$ 342,694	$ 128,363	$ (5,013)	$ 59,338	$ 767,253	4%
Other Income & Sales of Service	$ 569,691	$ 244,594	$ 70,110	$ 1,471,372	$ 66,856	$ 2,422,623	12%
	$ 11,960,585	$ 1,299,212	$ 4,133,902	$ 1,480,852	$ 893,130	$ 19,767,681	100%
Distribution by FUND	61%	7%	21%	7%	5%	100%	

Source: Financial Information of Universities and Colleges, 1989-90 and 2003-04, Table 2.1.A (Research Fund refers to consolidated entities only). In addition to the income shown in Table 1, universities also receive donations (and matching grants in some cases) for endowments. In FY90 that figure was approximately $90 million. In FY04 that figure was approximately $250 million.

---

[22] In fact the reduction is actually greater but has been masked by changes in the operating fund definition.

The preceding 'shifts' in income TYPE and FUND represent a major change in the evolution of university finances from more discretion and support of core operations to considerably less discretion and support for specific purposes. Moreover, funding changes in certain FUNDS actually have impacts in other FUNDS. For example, increases in research funding (and activity) carry with them increased demands on institutional infrastructure – sometimes referred to as 'indirect' costs. Until recently the federal granting councils provided grants to university faculty for specific research projects but the grants made no provision for 'indirect' costs, such as facilities upkeep, utilities, administrative support, library, and information technology support – all services that a researcher would be expected to use in his/her research work.[23] Accordingly, as research expanded over the period the increased research activity actually resulted in increased costs that were not being recognized through the federal granting councils. Those costs were being borne by the operating fund – funded largely by student tuition fees and provincial grants. The significant increase in research funding has fuelled a major increase in research activity and added an expanded mandate to many universities and some colleges.

The preceding analysis has focused on the university sector to illustrate some of the complexities associated with post-secondary funding and to highlight the major shift in emphasis – an expanded mandate – in research.

3.5. PSE Income: Changes in Income

Returning to the PSE sector as a whole, and the total funding of $27.7 billion cited previously, Figure 2 provides an illustration of the primary sources of funding and the legend provides a brief description of the major purposes of the funding.

---

[23] Beginning in 2001/02, the federal government began providing a provision to help with indirect costs. Initially a one-time allocation, the funding was formally committed on an on-going basis the following year. Initially pegged at $200 million the allocation is now $260 million (2005/06) and represents approximately 25 percent of indirect costs – a marked improvement but still a considerable distance from the 40 percent figure that is often cited as the minimum estimate of actual indirect costs.

Figure 2: Total Funding to Colleges and Universities by Source (2005)

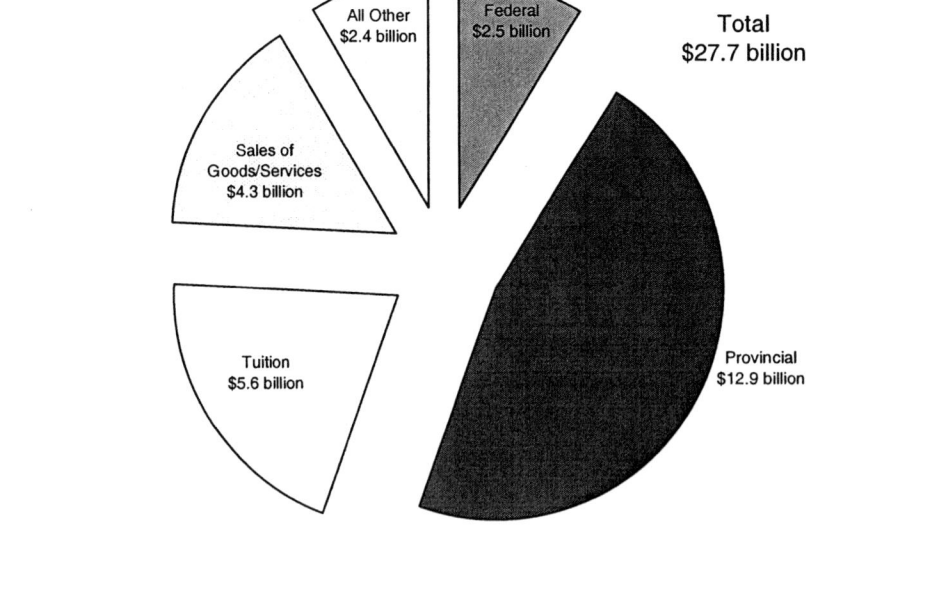

☐ Federal (primarily research)
☐ Tuition ('core operations' and some student assistance)
☐ All Other (student assistance and research with some 'core' and capital)
■ Provincial (primarily 'core' operations but includes capital and research)
☐ Sales of Goods/Services (ancillary services and contract research)

Statistics Canada, Financial Management System

Table 2 uses the same categorization of revenue to illustrate the change in those major sources of funding since the early 1990s.

Table 2 Total Funding to Colleges and Universities by Source 1992/93 – 2004/5 ($ billions)

	1992/93	%	2004/5	%
Federal (primarily research)	$ 1.1	7%	$ 2.5	9%
Provincial (primarily 'core' operations but includes capital and research)	$ 10.1	62%	$ 12.9	47%
Tuition ('core operations' and some student assistance)	$ 2.1	13%	$ 5.6	20%
Sales of Goods/Services (ancillary services and contract research)	$ 1.9	12%	$ 4.3	16%
All Other (student assistance and research with some 'core' and capital)	$ 1.2	7%	$ 2.4	9%
Total	$ 16.4	100%	$ 27.7	100%

Each of the pieces of the pie are reviewed in the following section, beginning with government post-secondary expenditures – which also includes reference to additional government expenditures beyond those made directly to colleges and universities.

a. Total Government Expenditures on Higher Education

Estimates of total government expenditure on higher education in Canada approach $20 billion.[24] About 75 percent of that expenditure occurs in the institutions (colleges and universities) as noted in Figure 2 above. However, a significant and growing portion is directly related to transfers or payments to individuals in the form of government student assistance, tax expenditures such as the education tax credit and the tuition tax credit, and government payments to the Canada Education Savings Grant. Since 1995 the increase in payments to individuals has increased dramatically and was estimated at over $4 billion – twice the amount, in real terms, than in 1990.[25] The vast majority of that increase is due to increased tax benefits introduced by the federal government from the mid-90's onwards – credits that resulted in tax expenditures at the provincial level as well.

Those transfers to individuals are important because they are often lost sight of when considering higher education finance. Yet, they represent – in the case of the federal government – deliberate decisions that affect the total 'cost' of higher education to the taxpayer. Further, because of the link between federal and provincial tax regimes, the federal decision has a major impact on provincial finances and, in some cases, is yet another contributor to federal/provincial acrimony. Moreover, a tax benefit represents a resource allocation decision by government – and the decision to use the tax system as an allocation device needs to be looked at in the context of other funding mechanisms the government could have employed (e.g., transfers to provinces and then from provincial coffers to universities/colleges, direct transfers to institutions, direct transfers to students such as loan subsidies and/or grants).

In addition to the preceding tax expenditures, it appears that governments are now transferring in the order of $15 billion per year (see Figure 2) directly to universities and colleges in the form of operating grants, capital grants, research grants and some funding for scholarships. As noted earlier, the past fifteen years is marked by two distinct periods – retrenchment from the early 90s to the mid-90s – and then expansion and re-investment from the latter part of the decade onwards. In the *Price of Knowledge 2004*, Junor and Usher catalogued the trend in direct **government** expenditures on universities and colleges since 1990. While they note that their methodology is "admittedly imperfect", it helps illustrate the periods of retrenchment and expansion and also illustrates the difference between federal spending and provincial spending. Figure 3 – a replica of Figure 5C.V.5 in that report – shows the peaking of provincial government expenditures in 1992, a period of slow decline with sharp reductions in 1996, the beginning of an upward turn in 1998 and funding increases essentially outpacing inflation since that point. At the federal level, the pattern is essentially the same although the expansionary period could be characterized as more robust. For the most part, the federal monies are for sponsored research while much of the provincial funding is for operating support.

---

[24] Junor, S. and Usher, A. *The Price of Knowledge 2004: Access and Student Finance in Canada*, The Canada Millennium Scholarship Foundation, 2004.
[25] Ibid., Figure 5C.VI.1 p. 269.

Figure 3: Total Government Expenditures on Post-Secondary Institutions
(in 2003 Real Dollars)

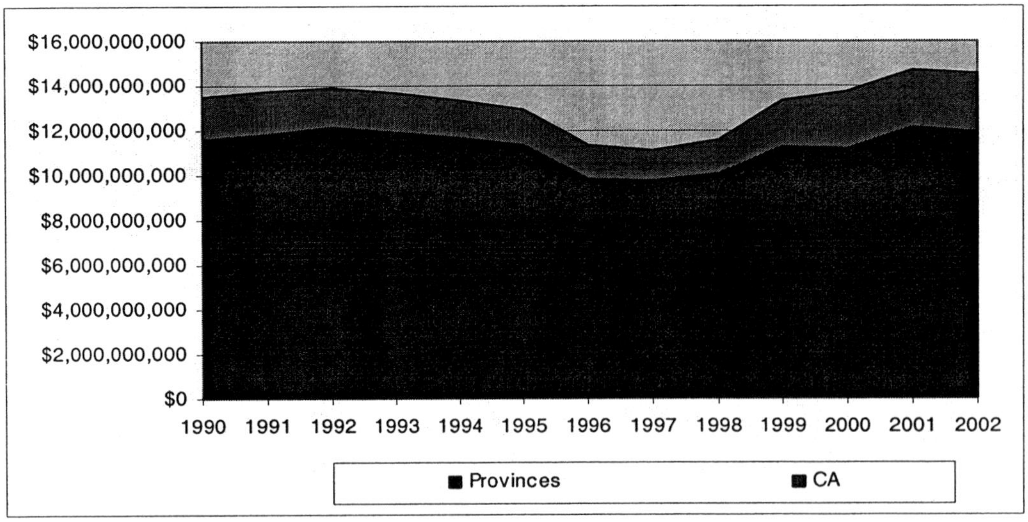

Source: *The Price of Knowledge 2004*, Figure 5C.V.5

b. Provincial Funding

Provincial grants tend to be used for operating support as well as capital, although some provinces also make significant investments in research. Figure 4 focuses on the provinces and, in light of the major differences in scale of operations, employs an index to normalize the changes in **provincial government** expenditure on post-secondary institutions. The dispersion in more recent times highlights the differences in provincial funding trends.

In general, the provinces decreased grants at some point in the early to mid parts of the 1990s, followed by a levelling off or expansion as the decade progressed. But, the differences are significant. While Alberta and Ontario experienced sharp drops that bottomed out at about 80 percent of the 1990 level, Newfoundland and Nova Scotia experienced a longer decline that bottomed out at a lower level. And the re-investment is significantly different in scale with Alberta and BC leading the way in terms of relative increases in provincial grants, a trend that has continued to the present and been reinforced through recent Budget announcements.[26] Readers should note that the inclusion of capital funding creates a discontinuity in the data – especially with respect to Ontario where the government invested approximately $1 billion in 1999 to begin preparations for the "double cohort".

---

[26] The Ontario situation appears to have improved in more recent years as well, first as a response to the 'double cohort' of graduating secondary school students (as a result of eliminating the 5th year of secondary school) and second in response to the (Rae) Post-secondary Review.

Figure 4: Indexed (relative to 1990 base year) Post-secondary Provincial Grants (in 2003 Real Dollars) (operating, capital, research)

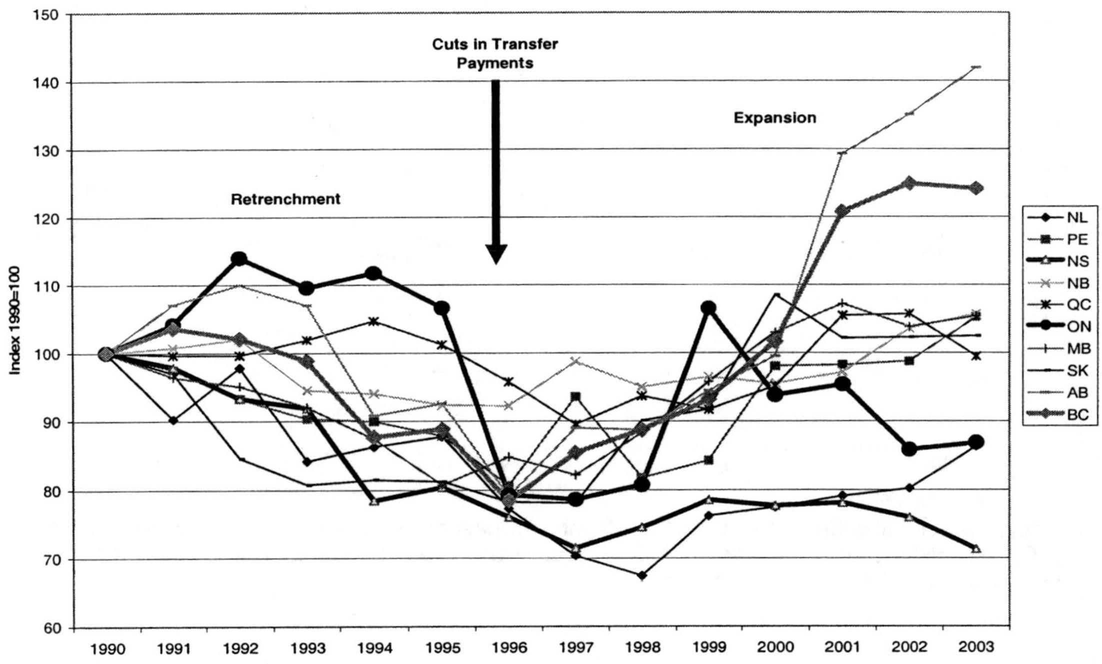

Source: *The Price of Knowledge 2004* Data Table 5C.V.5

Why the different trends in provincial government expenditure? Provincial funding to colleges and universities is a function of a multitude of factors including the state of provincial finances, competing demands, public finance philosophy, and politics. Yet, as David Foot has argued "Demographics explain about two-thirds of everything."[27] Whether a province's 18-19-year-old cohort is growing, holding steady, or declining may have a significant impact on demand for post-secondary education, institutional admission and enrolment policies, and ultimately a province's penchant for post-secondary education investment. Figure 5 provides the demographic picture for 18-19-year-olds across the country – the age group that historically considered post-secondary education. Those changes in the size of the 18-19 age group had a major impact on actual enrolment change as depicted in Figure 5.

---

[27] D.K Foot, *Boom Bust Echo 2000*, Macfarlane, Walter & Ross, Toronto, 1996 p.9

Figure 5: Indexed Change in the Number of 18-19-year-olds by Province (1990=100)

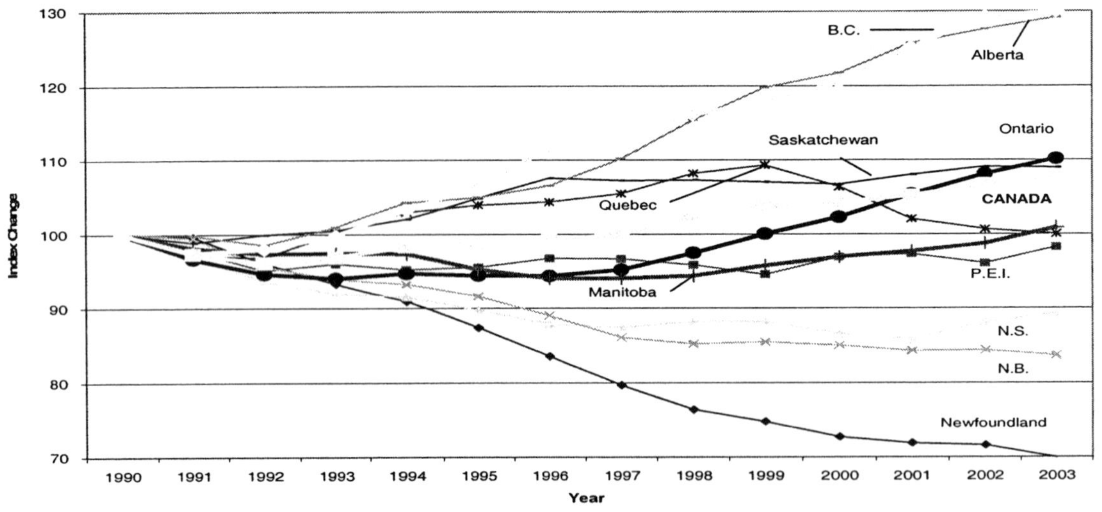

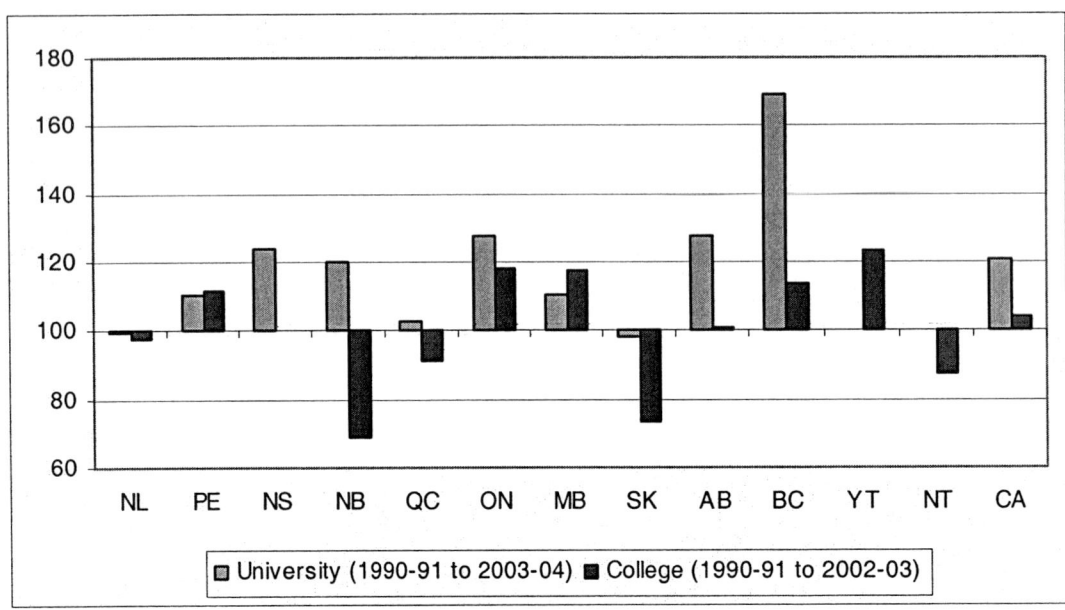

Source: Association of Universities and Colleges of Canada, based on 2001 census update as reported in Snowdon, K., *Applicant Data in Canada: Another Perspective on Access*, Canada Millennium Scholarship Foundation, December 2004

Figure 6: Changes in Enrolment by Province

Source: *The Price of Knowledge 2004* Data Figure 2.II.2.

The key messages from Figures 4, 5, and 6 are that prior to the mid-1990s the 18-19 year cohort was declining nationally, relative to 1990, with some notable exceptions. From 1998 onwards, however, the size of the 18-19 year cohort surpassed 1990 levels nationally. The arrival of the 'echo boom' appears to have had a marked impact on provincial funding in most provinces –

especially when coupled with increased participation rates that added further enrolment pressure. Whether demographics actually explains "two-thirds" or not, it is clear that demographics had a major impact. But, there are other factors that need to be considered as well.

In the first part of the retrenchment period some governments (Alberta and Ontario) cut provincial operating grants in the face of impending federal cut-backs but also as part of a program aimed at reducing the size of government, reflecting what has been termed a neo-liberal perspective. In the expansionary period a number of factors besides demographic pressures offer a plausible explanation for the reinvestment of public funds including a renewed interest in the economic importance of higher education; the relatively improved fiscal fortunes of the provinces and the presence of federal research funding that often required 'matching' contributions from the provinces/institutions.

c. Federal Funding

As noted earlier, federal funding was reduced sharply through cut-backs in federal transfer payments to the provinces. In the case of Ontario, for example, the recent Post-secondary Review estimated that the federal transfer for post-secondary education had decreased by about $550 million in real terms from 1992-93 to 2002-03.[28] In its place the federal government increased research funding, increased student assistance and provided tax expenditures that actually totalled more than the decrease in the federal transfer. But, the federal monies were delivered directly to institutions and individuals rather than through the province.

Figure 7: Federal Grants and Contracts in Canadian Universities

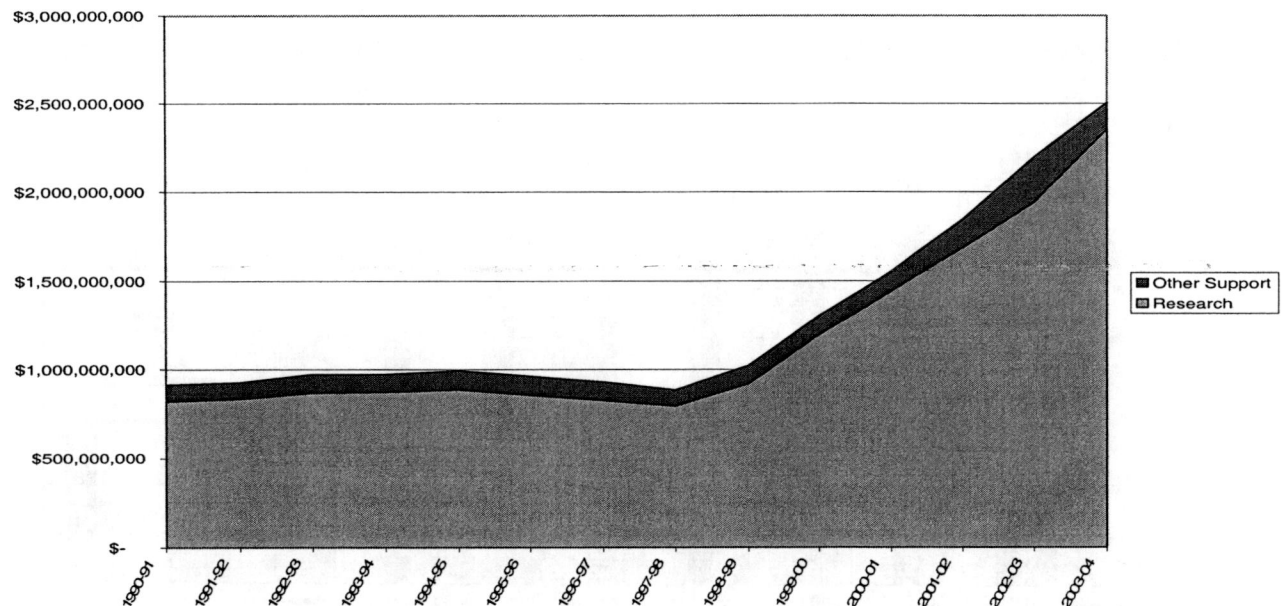

Source: CAUBO, Financial Statistics of Universities and Colleges

---

[28]Hon. Bob Rae, op.cit., p.96

The amount of increased research funding from the federal government is significant and has increased markedly since the mid-1990s as illustrated in Figure 7 which focuses solely on universities. From a reduced base of about $900 million in 1997-98, direct federal spending to the universities – largely in the form of research support – mushroomed to $2.5 billion. The significant increase in funding is one part of the equation in trying to understand the impact of the research investment; the others are the mechanisms the federal government chose to allocate the research funds and eligibility criteria for accessing the funds, matters we will return to in the funding mechanisms section.

d. Other Sources of Revenue

Tuition

As noted previously, federal and provincial grants are important components of university and college revenues. Universities and colleges also rely on other sources, notably tuition. In the university sector tuition income now accounts for about 32 percent of **operating** income nationally compared to about 16 percent in 1990 – that is, the proportion has doubled as illustrated in Figure 8 (Table 1 previously also showed a 'doubling' as a proportion of **total** income from 11 percent to 22 percent in the university sector).

The major increase in tuition in all provinces during the 1990s can be seen as two things: a reaction to cut-backs in federal transfers (the so-called "path of least resistance" according to one major study)[29] and an attempt, or experiment, to move towards a more market-based approach to funding higher education. However, it is obvious there were (and are) differing viewpoints about the 'share' of educational costs to be borne by students and their families. We return to the differences in tuition by province later in the paper when reviewing the regulatory environment.

Figure 8: Tuition and Fees as percent of Operating and Trust Income* (1990 and 2004)

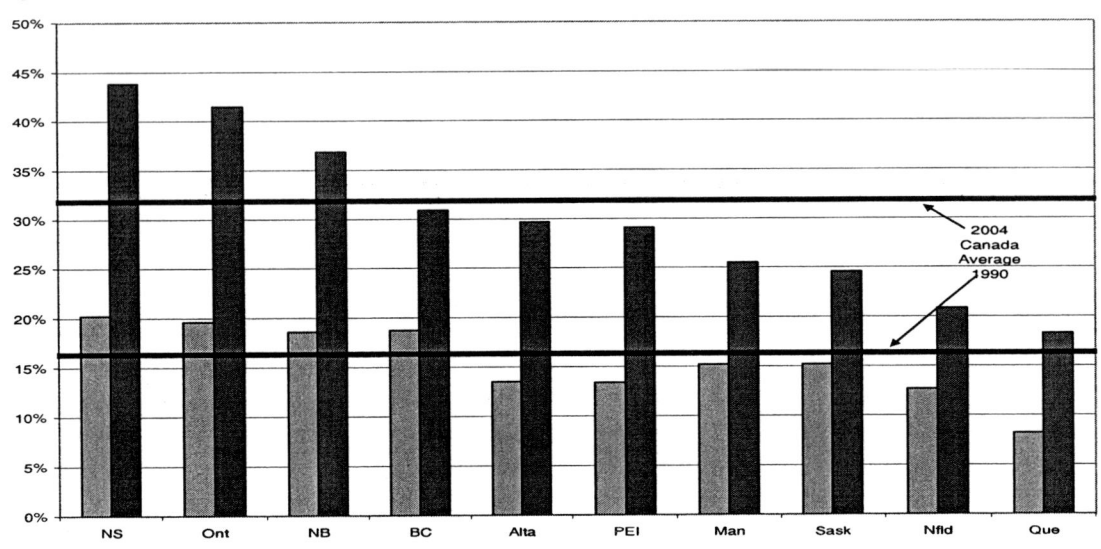

Source: 1989/90 and 2003/04 Financial Statistics Table 2.1.A
* To improve the comparability of the financial data among the provinces and reporting changes, the Operating and Trust Funds have been combined.

---

[29] H. Mackenzie, *Funding Post-secondary Education in Ontario: Beyond the Path of Least Resistance*, The Ontario Coalition for Post-secondary Education, December 2004.

Other Income
Another major change in the composition of funding is the increased presence of donations and investment income reflected in Figure 2 and Table 2 under "All Other". Those sources of funding are important components of the overall funding equation but, as noted previously, a donation often carries specific restrictions on its use. Investment income is susceptible to the vagaries of the market. For the most part 'Other income' is used to support student assistance (bursaries, scholarships), research chairs, and help finance capital construction.

Sales of Goods and Services
This category of revenue is linked directly to the provision of ancillary services such as residences, food services, bookstores, and parking facilities, as well as contract research. As noted previously ancillary services are managed on a break-even or for profit basis. As a proportion of total revenue, the sales of goods and services has increased due to the increase in contract research.

In summary, the funding trends since the early 1990s indicate that:

1) Total funding to colleges and universities is currently below 1992-93 levels in 6 of 10 provinces, after adjusting for enrolment and inflation (CPI);
2) The first half of the period was characterized by government restraint and cut-backs and measures were taken to look for other sources of revenue. The second half has been characterized by a funding expansion, fuelled initially by federal research monies and more recently by provinces reacting to increased access demands driven by the 'baby-boom echo' and increased participation rates; and
3) There have been major shifts in the sources of funding and, because of that added complexity, the overall increase in funding may not be quite what it seems on the surface. The funding is not being applied to a single purpose. Rather there are a multiplicity of purposes and often competing purposes. The PSE sector has evolved from a focus on teaching and education to an expanded mandate on research and innovation and more direct links to labour force training in support of provincial and federal economic goals. In the process the funding requirements and complexities have increased significantly.

e. Institutional Impacts

The shift in funding sources has not affected institutions equally. The Financial data from Table 1 provided the *average* distribution of funding by TYPE and FUND but there are wide variations around the average. For institutions in provinces where tuition increases were intended to help offset decreases in provincial grants, it follows that institutions with a greater reliance on tuition as a source of income would have a better *relative* situation than those institutions with a greater reliance on operating grants. However as institutions took steps to replace provincial monies with other sources – tuition, donations, research grants and contracts – the impacts were often not quite what was expected. Tuition increases carried with them increased obligations for student assistance – sometimes mandated by government but also often mandated by Boards of Governors. Institutions that moved to increase private giving soon realized that they had to make major investments in fund-raising infrastructure. Institutions that pushed to take advantage of expanded federal research funding soon recognized the reality of indirect costs. The fact is institutions adopted different approaches to diversify their revenue streams in the face of provincial funding cut-backs and constraints. Some institutions were able to transform excess university property into revenue-generating businesses and developments. Others were able to rely on existing endowment funds to help offset some of the grant reductions. Others were able to take advantage of actuarial pension surpluses to reduce pension contributions. And others were able to implement multi-year budgeting and planning strategies to 'smooth' the gyrations associated with government funding and regulatory changes. Every institution has an interesting, and different, story to tell, a reminder of the diversity that is an integral characteristic of the post-secondary sector.

4. Funding Comparisons

The preceding provides a brief overview of funding trends and the major changes in funding composition but says nothing about Canada's relative position to other jurisdictions. Attempts have been made to compare the PSE situation in Canada with the United States and progress continues to ensure that the comparisons are truly 'apples to apples'. But, in the same way there are major differences among the provinces in Canada, it is important to recognize there are significant differences *among* the states in the United States as evidenced in the following:

> Comparing institutions and states in expenditures per FTE student is a difficult task. States are different from each other. They have different climates, energy costs, housing costs, population densities, growth rates, and degrees of economic diversification. Some have a relatively homogenous, well-educated population, while others have large numbers of disadvantaged minorities and recent immigrants. Most states have pockets of poverty; these vary in their extent and concentration. State higher education systems also differ; some have many small institutions, some a few large institutions, some have more privately controlled ("independent") institutions, and some have more research universities, community colleges, or four-year universities. Across states, tuition policies and rates vary, as do the amounts and types of financial aid. Some institutions offer high-cost medical education and/or engineering programs, while others provide substantially more funding for research.[30]

In terms of trying to compare the Canadian post-secondary sector with the United States it has been argued that not only are the post-secondary systems different across the country but in the case of colleges:

> the reality is that the substantial variation among college systems within each country makes comparison at the national level problematic. For example, in some ways community colleges in Alberta are more like those in Florida than like colleges in Ontario. And colleges in Louisiana have been more like those in Ontario than those in Florida.[31]

One could make similar arguments about the difficulty of trying to compare universities in Canada and the United States. Nevertheless, there appears to be evidence of a funding 'gap' between Canadian post-secondary institutions and their counterparts in the United States.

> The reality is that, in comparison to four-year public universities in our major competitor country, the United States, Canadian universities are increasingly at a disadvantage. The former now receive C$5,000 more per student from governments than do Canadian universities. The additional resources at U.S. institutions are being used for teaching, student support services, libraries, research and public services –

---

[30] State Higher Education Executive Officers, State Higher Education Finance 2004, Making Sense of Interstate Higher Education Finance Data: Valid Comparisons – More or Less, SHEEO 2005.

[30] Michael L. Skolnik, *The Relationship of the community college to other providers of post-secondary and adult education in Canada and implications for policy*, Higher Education Perspectives, Volume 1, No. 1, 2004

the types of investments that enhance the quality of the learning environment for students.

This type of quality learning environment is highly correlated to student learning and personal development, as well as to the development of highly valued skills in a knowledge economy.[32]

In its research and policy analysis efforts, the Council of Ontario Universities (COU) conducts research into jurisdictional funding comparisons. In its most recent report COU estimated a funding 'gap' of approximately $5,000-$6,000 per student between Ontario institutions and a set of peer institutions in the United States.[33]

The Ontario Task Force on Competitiveness, Productivity and Economic Progress reported that the revenue gap between Ontario's universities and public universities in a set of 'peer' states was about $2,900 per student adjusted for purchasing parity and about double that amount based on an exchange rate conversion.[34] Put another way, the Task Force indicated that total college expenditure in Ontario was 68 percent of the U.S. level and total university expenditure was about 57 percent of the U.S. level.[35]

Regardless of the comparison and, notwithstanding difficulties in trying to ensure an 'apples to apples' funding comparison, the resource gap noted above appears to be significant. Universities and colleges have drawn attention to that gap before but the verification of it by third-parties like the Ontario Task Force on Competitiveness, Productivity and Economic Progress, and the linking of the higher education gap to the 'productivity gap' has helped translate the implications of the higher education funding gap into a more easily understood economic argument. When coupled with the 'push' of demographics and increasing awareness of the economic benefits from investments in research and innovation, the gap has helped some provinces and the federal government better understand and rationalize the increased PSE investments.

Another jurisdiction that has garnered attention more recently is the United Kingdom, where major initiatives are underway to re-invest in higher education. According to the Higher Education White Paper, the *Future of Higher Education*, "funding per student fell 36 percent between 1989 and 1997"[36] a pattern not dissimilar from that experienced in Canada over the same period.[37] The production of the White Paper marked a major turning point in the public commitment to PSE and since 2003 the UK has embarked on a major re-investment to improve quality, expand access and increase research. Given that per student funding levels in the U.K. were reported to be higher than in Canada[38] one can surmise that the more recent initiatives in

---

[32] Claire M. Morris and Robert Best, *Notes for a Presentation to the House of Commons Standing Committee on Finance*, June 13, 2005, Association of Universities and Colleges of Canada.
[33] Council of Ontario Universities, *Resource Document 2004*, July 2004, Table 2.6
[34] Hon. Bob Rae, op.cit., p.94
[35] Task Force on Competitiveness, Productivity and Economic Progress, *Realizing our prosperity potential*, Third Annual Report, November 2004. p. 24
[36] Department for Education and Skills, *Future of Higher Education*, United Kingdom, 2003. Executive Summary http://www.dfes.gov.uk/hegateway/strategy/hestrategy/foreword.shtml
[37] AUCC, *Trends in Higher Education*, Association of Universities and Colleges of Canada, 2002 p.65.
[38] Ibid.

the U.K. will lead to a continued funding advantage. However, what the U.K. government has set out to do in its White Paper and what it actually *does* bears continuing monitoring.[39]

Jurisidictional comparisons are fraught with problems and pitfalls and it is not easy to drill below national 'averages' to determine better funding comparisons that take into account differences in program 'mix', mission, and the level of undergraduate, professional, masters and doctoral enrolments within an institution, state or country. Some efforts have been made to focus on 'peer comparisons' and those more detailed studies (COU) provide a more in-depth glimpse of funding differences. However, in general, considerably more effort is required to arrive at better comparative information that would provide a higher level of confidence the comparisons are truly 'apples to apples'.

---

[39] For more information about funding in the U.K. please see http://www.universitiesuk.ac.uk/statistics/funding/

5. Funding Mechanisms

5.1. Characteristics of Funding Mechanisms in Canada

As an allocation device, the design of the funding mechanism is important if it is to be used to allocate funds in an acceptable fashion (acceptable to government and acceptable to the institutions). Some key considerations in assessing the efficacy of the allocation *mechanism* follow:[40]

- Equity – the allocation mechanism (formula) should strive to achieve equitable allocations based on common quantifiable factors (i.e., enrolment, physical inventory)
- Predictability – allocation mechanism (formula) should allow for a high degree of predictability in overall funding.
- Stability – allocation mechanism (formula) should provide smooth transitions to major year to year changes in funding distribution and allocation.
- Accountability – through the use of simple inputs (i.e., enrolment) the allocation mechanism (formula) should provide an easy to understand *part* of the accountability framework. For example if the funding formula is based on the number of enrolled students, it automatically incorporates an accountability component that is easy to understand: institutions get paid for the number of students enrolled. Of course that should be augmented by outcome reports, public financial reporting, and the easy availability of measures that can be used to determine if the funds are achieving intended objectives.
- Simplicity/Transparency– allocation mechanism (formula) should be easy to explain and understand and the factors that trigger changes in allocations should have a clear rationale.

If allocation mechanism(s) incorporate the preceding considerations in the design, it is likely – notwithstanding expressed concerns about the *level* of funding – that the allocation mechanism will help achieve the goal associated with the funding or at least be neutral with respect to influencing institutional behaviours. However, it is by no means guaranteed for a variety of reasons. First, the concept of equity can be, as noted by David Cameron in his review of the funding formula in Nova Scotia, "straightforward in concept and beguilingly elusive in its practical import."[41] Cameron then notes that equity has two components and he cites from Stefan Dupre's funding reviews in Alberta and British Columbia:

> An equitable condition in the public financing of universities can be deemed to exist when those in similar situations are treated similarly and those in different situations are treated in a manner commensurate with their differences.[42]

---

[40] The listing of considerations is intended to be illustrative and taken from variety of documents including the annual reports of the Ontario Council on University Affairs (various years) and the Saskatchewan Universities Funding Review (1998).

[41] D. Cameron, Equity and purpose in financing universities: The case of Nova Scotia, *Canadian Public Administration*, Vol. 43, No.3. p. 297

[42] Ibid., p. 298

The "rub" according to Cameron, is trying to determine which differences are to be recognized and by how much. For example, some funding systems recognize the additional costs associated with remote service delivery or geographic remoteness, but where do you draw the line? Should universities and colleges in large urban centres be compensated for differences in the cost-of-living versus institutions in lower cost areas? Another example could be providing special grants for the differences associated with resource-intensive research (i.e., 'big science') that demand significant infrastructure and operating costs – but how do you define 'big science'?

Second, the allocation mechanism may not be appropriate to respond to *major* shifts in resources or demands – upwards or downwards. In times of major enrolment expansion (or decline) and major resource expansion (or constraint) other actions may be required to transition to a new 'steady state'. For example, in Ontario the elimination of the 5th year of secondary school would have resulted in a major reduction in funding to School Boards under the existing Student Focused Funding model. To counter that impact, the government introduced a special envelope to smooth the effect of enrolment declines. Similarly, in the same province, the same phenomenon led to a suspension of part of the existing funding formula for universities because the significant increase in enrolment in one year played havoc with the calculation of moving averages, intended to smooth impacts.

Third, the allocation mechanism is premised on an assumption that there is a goal – a well understood, reasonably articulated goal or, at the very least, a clear purpose for the use of the funds. The evolving roles of universities and colleges and the multiple roles they are expected to fulfil make the establishment of specific goals or purposes more difficult. The introduction of more earmarked funding was an attempt to address specific goals but a particular allocation mechanism must be seen within the whole funding picture.

And finally, even the best allocation mechanism will have limited impact on achieving goals if, in fact, the means are simply inadequate – a characteristic of much of the period under discussion.

The characteristics of the funding mechanism are important but the process for developing and implementing a funding mechanism is critical as well – is it forced, arrived at after consultation, or arrived at as a joint response? In that regard the period from 1990 onwards could be described as raucous and rancorous. As some provincial governments moved to introduce new funding mechanisms there was a noticeable lack of consultation and review of policy options with the sector. At the same time it appears that some of the federal initiatives suffered from lack of consultation with the provinces and/or institutions. Not only did the lack of consultation affect the intended outcome but the process, especially against a backdrop of neo-liberalism, was often interpreted in the worst possible light by many stakeholders in the post-secondary sector. In a recent book about federal/provincial relations, the opening chapter, *Trust In Intergovernmental Fiscal Relations*,[43] chronicles the demise of 'trust' in federal-provincial relations and makes a sound case for the importance of rebuilding trust. The same message could, of course, apply to relationships between the post-secondary sector and a number of provincial governments.

---

[43] Lazar, H., *Canadian Fiscal Arrangements: What Works What Might Work Better*, McGill-Queen's Press, 2005

5.2. Provincial Funding Mechanisms

Appendix B provides a review of the actual provincial funding mechanisms in play across the country at the college and university levels with an emphasis on the mechanism used to distribute core operating grants. Three points emerge from the review of funding mechanisms over the period: first, the funding mechanisms are allocation devices, that is the total amount of government funding in the sector is set by government not driven by the funding mechanism; second, in many provinces the funding mechanisms have been altered over the last fifteen years, to varying degrees, to introduce more earmarked funding through special funding envelopes; and third, a number of governments adopted deliberate policies to leverage specific funding allocations by requiring matching contributions – specifically for infrastructure investment and student assistance endowment.

Another observation is relevant; in some provinces (and at the federal level) the government used, or attempted to use, the funding mechanism(s) to steer universities and colleges towards greater competition and improved performance as defined by government. At the provincial level, those efforts have evolved more recently towards greater emphasis on outcomes as delineated in performance contracts, service plans, and various agreements between the province and its post-secondary partners. The shift, over time, reflects the retrenchment/expansion phases noted earlier. During the retrenchment period and for the early part of the re-investment period, some governments were very interventionist, attempting to restructure post-secondary education and force efficiencies. Budget constraint was the order of the day. Inflation was ignored and new monies were only available for specific programs/projects – through earmarked grants. Once the expansion period was in full swing, however, governments seem to have embraced the cause, loosening purse strings a bit and showing much greater interest in multi-year planning agreements as a key instrument of accountability – although the penchant for intervention has not necessarily diminished.

Over the past fifteen years there have been significant changes in funding mechanisms in many provinces. Largely under the banner of accountability, more targeted funding envelopes were introduced, often requiring additional reporting. In some cases the additional funding envelopes were aimed at specific government initiatives (i.e., increased funding for disability services) or increased enrolment in specific programs (i.e., expanding teacher education, or medical enrolments). In other cases the funding envelope was intended to encourage and recognize performance differences and improvements in specific areas (i.e., employment rates, graduation rates). The absolute funding associated with these new envelopes varied and, in the case of 'performance funds', tended to represent one to two percent of the total. However, in the mid-90s those envelopes were essentially the only new government monies available and there was considerable uncertainty about whether the 'envelope' approach would subsume the existing funding mechanisms. That level of uncertainty influenced the PSE environment in a generally negative fashion.

In light of the new funding mechanisms that were introduced, the end result for institutions was, generally, less predictability, less stability, more reporting, and confusion about the intent and application of the earmarked funding. In commenting on a performance funding initiative in Ontario, for example, Lang noted that "the performance funding cum performance indicators program changed four times in eight years."[44] While rooted in a belief that consumers (students) needed more and better information to make decisions about post-secondary education choices – a laudable goal – the performance indicator initiative in Ontario was soon transformed into an allocation scheme that was seen as punitive in application and dismissive of local circumstance and differentiation. Did it change institutional behaviours? Likely not, because the measures were crude, outside the direct influence of the institutions, and the funding was not only inadequate to finance improvement but also subject to annual fluctuations and thus less than conducive to supporting on-going improvement initiatives. Did it help inform prospective students? Evidence from the College Applicant Survey indicates that Key Performance Indicator results are ranked very low in terms of influencing college choice although there appears to a bit higher interest among prospective students from low income households.[45]

The Ontario experience was not unique. Alberta had its own 'Performance Envelope' that suffered from design and implementation flaws[46] and currently has nine separate indicators as follows:

- enrolment growth;
- satisfaction of recent graduates;
- employment of recent graduates;
- administration expenditure efficiency;
- revenue generation through entrepreneurial activities;
- sponsored research awards;
- citation impact of research papers;
- community and industry support of research activity; and
- revenue generation through research activity.[47]

A government-sponsored review of the Alberta funding regime found that the Performance Envelope, when all was said and done, was regarded – at least partially – more as an "adjustment intended to help offset general cost pressures than an award for performance."[48]

In a similar way, the various funds that governments provided for growth (targeted or untargeted) tended to be in lieu of any general increase in operating funding. And such funds tended to be tightly controlled, with a constant threat of funding penalties if an institution exceeded specific enrolment quotas or if the total enrolment increase exceeded the available government funding. On the one hand, it was a very effective way to induce institutions to take more students – no growth, no money. On the other hand the tight-fisted application was not driven by access considerations but rather expenditure control considerations. In reality, once inflation factored into the equation, institutions accepted additional students at marginal

---

[44] D.W. Lang, *The Political Economy of Performance Funding*, in Iacobucci and Tuohy, eds., Taking Public Universities Seriously, p. 242
[45] Acumen Research, *Ontario College Applicant Survey 2005, Canada Millennium Scholarship Foundation System Level Report*, Fall 2005.
[46] For a detailed description of the Alberta initiative, see D. Shale, *Alberta's performance based funding mechanism and Alberta universities*." Paper presented at the annual conference of the Canadian Institutional Research and Planning Association, 1999.
[47] Alberta Advanced Education, Quality in Alberta's Advanced Education System, July 2005, p.12
[48] Report of the MLA Post-secondary Funding Review Committee, Alberta, October 2000, p.21

operating grant levels (Alberta, Ontario). In that environment, the tuition associated with that additional student attracted considerable attention and, depending on a particular institution's specific circumstances, was a major factor in determining whether an institution would, in fact, expand its enrolment.

The formal introduction of the requirement for 'matching' funds or private sector contributions was another 1990s development that fit with some key precepts of neo-liberalism. By requiring private sector contributions or partners a province could limit its own expenditure, provide an external 'market' check, shift funding responsibility to the private sector and still produce the required product or service. In Ontario, for example, the strategy initially appeared to work as intended – universities and colleges increased their fundraising capacity and began to forge closer links to business. Before long, the province of Ontario had adopted the leveraging concept as a mantra. Capital investments required major private sector contributions; to help universities and colleges improve student assistance funding over the longer term, the government provided matching funds to create endowments[49]; and the expansion of enrolments in engineering and computer science was aided by corporate contributions. Figure 9 illustrates the impact – a noticeable increase in donations that essentially levelled off around the year 2000 under the weight of the dot.com implosion and what was called 'donor fatigue'.

---

[49] It is important to note that non-expendable donations (endowments) yield, on average, approximately 4-5 percent in annual expendable income. Thus, while important, the actual annual spending levels are relatively modest.

Figure 9: Donations to Ontario Universities

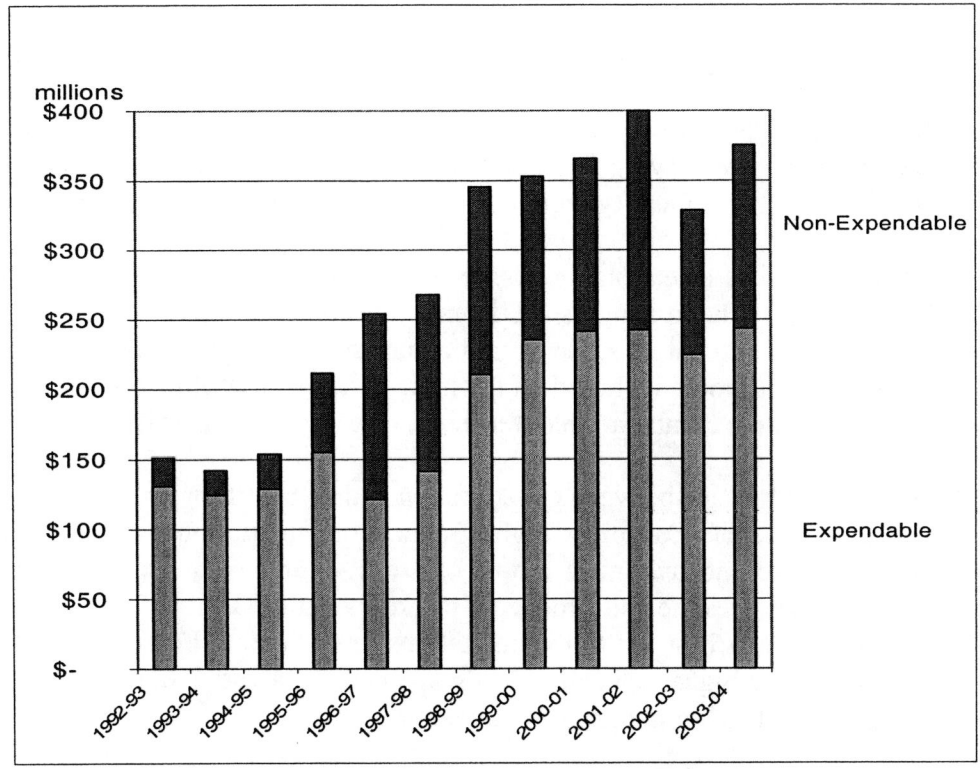

Source: Committee of Finance Officers – Universities of Ontario, Financial Report of Ontario Universities, Supplementary Volume and Council of Ontario Universities, Resource Document 2004.

The initial success of relying on more private funding gave way to the realization on many campuses that raising money was hard work, required a significant investment in appropriate infrastructure and, increasingly, required a considerable investment of time by faculty and senior administrators. Perhaps more importantly, private fund-raising moved from being a source of funding to provide the "margin of excellence" in a predominantly government funded/controlled system to becoming a regular source of funding, often replacing previous government investment.

The penchant for earmarked funding and relying on more private funding was occurring at the same time that increases in core funding were essentially negligible. Institutions had little recourse but to 'play the game' because earmarked funding was essentially the 'only game in town'. Further, in 'playing the game' there was considerable concern that all the rules were in the hands of the government and they could (and would) change them at any time.[50]

It is instructive to reflect on the nature of competition in higher education because the move to more earmarked funding and greater reliance on market mechanisms (i.e., tuition) seemed to be

---

[50] For examples in Ontario, see K. Snowdon, *Assessing the Revenue Framework and Multi-year Planning in Ontario: A Leader in Learning (Rae Report),* forthcoming.

premised on an assumption of limited or non-existent competition in higher education. The late David Smith spoke to the matter in his treatise on quality.

> Universities compete and should compete. They compete for the best faculty, the best students, the most funds, and the best learning environment. For all such attributes, "best" and "most" are defined by the nature of the institution and its mission, but there are varying degrees of overlap among institutions that strengthen competitive incentives. Quality requires that these incentives are sufficiently strong.
>
> Quality also requires a reasonable degree of collaboration among universities. This collaboration is to be distinguished from collusion that results in monopolistic practices to the detriment of students and other users of the services of universities. This collaboration should be based on the more effective use of resources that can be achieved through the combination of teaching, research and administrative matters.[51]

Striking the appropriate balance between collaboration and competition is not an easy task. There are numerous examples of Canadian higher education institutions sharing services and establishing collaborative endeavours in a host of areas – for resource reasons as well as the recognition that in some cases the end-product is markedly better. That competitive/collaborative balance, one might argue, is best left to the institutions to sort out.[52] Forced collaboration is not only an oxymoron, but the higher education landscape is littered with examples that would make great case studies for students of public administration.

The apparent desire for more competition also belies the actions of some governments. Competition leads to winners and losers: governments have a difficult time with winners and losers. Governments have ample opportunity to rely on the 'market' to allocate resources but they will often by-pass the competitive option for other considerations. A case in point is the recently announced expansion of 25,000 more post-secondary spaces in British Columbia. Government could simply fund 25,000 more spaces based on students 'voting with their feet' and institutions (colleges, universities and university-colleges) marketing their programs. Instead, the government made a decision to allocate the spaces based on a number of factors including, it appears, the regional economic development potential of expanded capacity. The point is governments 'talk' about wanting more competition but there are a number of considerations that actually influence government actions.

Similar arguments could be made about some federal research initiatives or competitions for a host of government monies at the provincial level. Governments, for a variety of reasons, will consider a variety of factors besides pure competition and market tests. In commenting on the CFI program and its requirement for matching funding, for example, Cameron notes that given the state of finances in the Atlantic region and the relatively limited availability of private funding, the federal government provided $300 million to

---

[51] Smith, op.cit., p.33
[52] An example of greater co-operation is the expansion of medical enrolment in British Columbia involving a partnership between UBC, University of Victoria and UNBC. See D. Fisher et al., *The Development of a Post-Secondary Education System in British Columbia: Transformation and Change*, unpublished draft paper, May 2005)

> the Atlantic Canada Opportunities Agency, a federal body responsible for economic development in the Atlantic region ... available specifically for the purpose of providing the funds necessary to contribute to the matching contribution required by the CFI.[53]

And so it goes, competition and the rigour of the market compromised by other realities.

One of those realities, in fact the single biggest reality, is the need to adhere to some semblance of equity in the distribution of public monies. At the margin, governments can allocate funding differentially and generally rationalize such allocations on the basis of specific circumstances (i.e., Northern Grants in the Ontario funding system). However, in terms of *core* operating funding it is very difficult for government to justify why the public subsidy for an undergraduate history student at the University of Saskatchewan, for example, should be different than the public subsidy for an undergraduate history student at the University of Regina. How could a government defend providing a different level of public subsidy for students in a similar program at two institutions in the same province? That notion of equity, by definition, means that allocating funding on the basis of competition will necessarily be a relatively small part of the overall funding equation. Otherwise, the forces of equity will prevail. And that, in fact, is what appears to have happened in provinces where additional emphasis was placed on variations of what might be considered "competitive funding". In Alberta, for example, the very first recommendation of the government's MLA Post-secondary Funding Review Committee was "Equity Adjustments to Base Grants."[54] In Ontario, Bob Rae made a point of noting that the "allocation of provincial operating grants will be equitable – students in similar programs at different institutions will receive similar funding from government."[55] The notion of equity in provincial grant funding is a characteristic of the funding mechanisms across the country. In some cases it is explicit in the establishment of formulas, in other cases it is implicit in funding practices. At the federal level, however, the notion of equity played out quite differently as we will see in the next section.

5.3. Federal Funding Mechanisms

As noted previously, the latter part of the 1990s and early years of the 21st century witnessed a major federal investment in research and research infrastructure not to mention renewed federal forays into student assistance. Cut-backs in direct funding to the provinces in the early to mid-90s were replaced with specific federal programs that exhibited characteristics of their own.

a. Federal Research Initiatives

In the case of research, the investments ran the gamut from new programs such as the Canada Foundation for Innovation, the Canada Research Chairs program and Indirect Costs to increased funding for the Granting Councils and the transformation of the Medical Research Council into the Canadian Institutes for Health Research. At the same time, to further bolster its Innovation Agenda, the Federal government introduced a major commitment to Graduate Scholarships. The

---

[53] Cameron, D., op.cit. p.282
[54] *Report of the MLA Post-secondary Funding Review Committee*, October, 2000 p.1
[55] Hon. Bob Rae, *Ontario: A Leader in Learning*, February 2005, pp. 96-97

result, as suggested by David Wolfe in commenting about the situation in Ontario, especially when

> combined with the introduction of new provincial programs, have greatly strengthened the research capacity of post-secondary institutions, including the research and teaching hospitals, within the province.[56]

A similar conclusion would, no doubt, be echoed by the university community across the country although it is important to note that the federal largesse did not necessarily fall evenly across the country nor across the array of institutions. In the process, the federal government put a firm stamp on its role in post-secondary education. The federal government and the university community (through AUCC) agreed to a framework agreement in 2002 that confirmed the universities acceptance of the various targets in the Innovation Strategy and committed the federal government to provide the necessary resources.[57] The provinces were notable by their absence.

The federal research initiatives had direct impacts on provincial coffers. The Canada Foundation for Innovation, for example, funded 40 percent of an approved project with the remainder to come from the province and the institution; local priorities were steered by the presence of federal monies. The indirect costs associated with federal research grants were not fully offset by the new allowances for such costs, so the rest still had to be financed from somewhere, usually by stretching straitened provincial and tuition resources that, ostensibly should have been used for teaching and coping with increased enrolment demand. Scholarships for more graduate students led to cries from the institutions to the provinces for more operating funds to provide the instruction, supervision and required services and facilities to expand graduate enrolment.

Not surprisingly, provinces became adept at factoring the impact of federal programs directly into their own equations. For example, the advent of federal indirect costs and the Canada Research Chairs program provided an opportunity for a province to recoup some of the funding it had been 'forced' to allocate to the post-secondary sector. Rather than provide additional funding for new faculty positions or general inflation, provinces could elect to 'tweak' their own allocations – and they did. And the individual institutions were even quicker to adopt the concept of resource substitution internally – even in the face of increased federal accountability requirements.

Yet another impact of the federal initiative was the steering of research to specific ends "to shift that research in favour of the applied, and especially patentable, end of the research scale."[58] Whether that meshed with provincial priorities (or whether a province had research priorities) was not a question the federal government seemed interested in asking. The same effect was felt by institutions where the CFI requirement for an institutional strategic research plan began driving other aspects of the institutional planning agenda such as facility requirements, faculty hiring, graduate enrolment, and fundraising.

---

[56] D. Wolfe, *Innovation and Research Funding: The Role of Government Support*, in Iacobucci and Tuohy, Op.cit., p.329
[57] D, Cameron, *Post-Secondary Education and Research: Whither Canadian Federalism?"* in Ibid., p.287
[58] Ibid., p.282

Finally, there was at least one other major impact associated with the significant increase in federal research funding: the steering effect on faculty time and workloads. The proliferation of programs created what has been referred to as "an extraordinary complexity of grant deadlines and opportunities"[59] that require a significant amount of faculty time.

> Our young investigators spend 30 percent or more of their time writing grants and rewriting the same grant; their colleagues spend another 30 percent of *their* time reviewing the grants that have been submitted.[60]

Neither of the preceding time allocations translate into actually doing the research. When the research work is factored into the equation it begins to be clear that a significant amount of faculty time is devoted to research activities. What is the effect on *educational* quality at the undergraduate level? Massy, in commenting on the situation in the United States, a decade ago, argued that the

> cross-pressures generated by sponsored research programs put more pressure on undergraduate teaching performance than the extra funding alleviates thorough contributions to the institution's fixed cost.[61]

If Massy's argument rings true in the United States, where there is considerably greater funding for indirect costs, it is even more likely to be true in Canada where rates for indirect costs are still a fraction of the rates in the United States.

The federal research programs have had another major impact: institutional differentiation. The decision to use 'research' as the focus of the federal investment in universities resulted in quite different allocation results than if the funds had flowed through the province and been distributed through the operating grants mechanism. By adopting the precepts of existing federal research funding mechanisms the notion of 'equity' played out quite differently at the institutional level. Federally, the granting councils had well-established allocation programs that, for the most part, were seen as using peer-adjudicated competitions to fund individual professors. The concept of competitive grants was part of the research ethos and the results, when 'rolled up' to the institutional level showed a quite different allocation result than if the monies were simply allocated, for example, on the basis of the number of faculty in each institution or as, noted previously, through the provincial operating grant mechanism. Since a major part of the re-investment of federal funds was in the form of increased funding to the granting councils, the existing emphasis on peer-adjudicated competition remained in place. To reinforce that further, the allocation of Canada Research Chairs was, essentially, based on institutional shares of the granting council research grants with a floor provision to ensure every institution received at least one Canada Research Chair. The allocation of indirect costs was also linked to total institutional research grants with an added 'capacity-building' provision for smaller institutions.

---

[59] J.Challis, et.al., *The University Research Environment*, in Iacobucci and Tuohy, Ibid., p. 368
[60] Ibid., p. 368
[61] W. Massy, *Measuring Performance: How Colleges and Universities Can Set meaningful Goals and Be Accountable*, in W.Massy and J. Meyerson, eds., *Measuring Institutional Performance in Higher Education*, Peterson's, Princeton, 1994. p.34

The result of the federal investments and the chosen allocation instruments is that institutions with a significant research presence – as measured by their share of federal granting council funding – benefited markedly. By virtue of federal funding initiatives involving billions of dollars a very small set of Canadian institutions emerged as the clear research leaders. Ironically, the provisions for smaller institutions fuelled greater interest in research among institutions that would have been traditionally regarded as teaching institutions and encouraged institutional aspirations far beyond existing capacities. Whether that is in the long term interest of higher education remains to be seen, but to expand the capacity of those institutions will require considerable *provincial* investment, yet another example of a federal initiative that has significant long-term consequences for individual provinces.

b. Federal Initiatives on Student Aid

In the case of federal student assistance, there were two key thrusts: improved tax benefits for individuals incurring post-secondary education costs; and direct investments in the form of improved bursaries and awards and incentives to encourage educational savings. Improved tax benefits include increased education and tuition tax credits and a new tax credit for student loan interest, as well as a major increase in the tax exemption for award income. The tax expenditure approach reflected the federal response to increased tuition (which one might argue was at least partly due to federal cut-backs in provincial grants) and has a number of characteristics that deserve comment.

First, the federal initiatives seem designed to put funds directly into the hands of the student (or family); the motives for doing so can be ascribed to a number of factors including a desire to improve the visibility of federal investments, ensure the federal monies ended up supporting post-secondary initiatives, and create a more market-oriented approach to purchasing post-secondary services by putting the dollars in the hands of the consumer and/or providing incentives for educational savings.

Second, the increased tax benefits (tax credits and tax exemptions) impact provincial finances in several ways because (with the exception of Quebec) the federal government collects income tax on behalf of the provinces and, until recently, provincial tax rates were set as a proportion of the federal rate. When the federal government introduced new tax credits the result was less federal *and* provincial income tax. The steering effect was not well received by some of the provinces and, when coupled with other federal/provincial tensions, ultimately led to the establishment of provincial tax credit regimes. At one time the post-secondary tax credits were uniform across the country (with the exception of Quebec). Now, the value of the credits varies by province.[62]

Third, the tax credit and tax exemption initiatives have put a new twist on the term 'student assistance' since individuals from all income levels benefit from the credits and deductions. The tax credit approach has been characterized as "poorly targeted" in that the credits "are distributed almost entirely without reference to need".[63] The Federal government reacted to that criticism

---

[62] See Chapter 5B, *Sources of Student Assistance* in Junor and Usher, *The Price of Knowledge, 2004*.
[63] Finnie, R., et al, *Meeting the Need: A New Architecture for Canada's Student Financial Aid System*, in Beach, C.M., et.al., *Higher Education in Canada*, p.503

by enhancing its needs-based Canada Student Loan Program and a number of provinces have, more recently, introduced further needs-based measures.

The establishment of the Canada Millennium Scholarship Foundation was the primary vehicle for the investment of bursaries and awards aimed at improving access and reducing student debt. Much has been written about the Foundation's efforts and is captured in a quote from David Cameron's "Post-secondary Education and Research: Whither Canadian Federalism?"

> . . . the foundation got itself tangled up in overlapping federal and provincial student aid arrangements, with the result that much of the federal bursaries simply displaced existing provincial student aid. The net benefit has been a good deal less than the federal contribution to the foundation.[64]

To the Foundation's credit, more recent arrangements with individual provinces point towards greater added benefit to individual students and a greater commitment of provincial funds.[65]

At one level the re-emergence of the federal presence in the higher education arena must be seen as a positive development, improving the state of research and the overall level of student assistance. At another level, those 'improvements' have been at the expense of other components of the higher education sector. The re-emergence of the federal presence coincided with a shift in the federal emphasis and the establishment of a set of funding mechanisms that have added greater complexity to the post-secondary landscape and led to increased friction in federal-provincial relations. Universities, colleges and their students have had to deal with the impacts.

---

[64] Cameron, D., op.cit., p. 283
[65] See for example a new joint program in New Brunswick for low-income students and new programs in other provinces at http://www.millenniumscholarships.ca/en/newsevents/PressReleases.asp

6. The Regulatory Environment: Tuition, Degree-granting and Accountability

The period from 1990 to the present is marked by major changes in tuition policy in many provinces and major changes in degree granting policies in some provinces. Guided by an adoption of neo-liberal policies (as defined previously) various governments moved to make the higher education sector more market responsive and chose tuition policy and degree granting policy as prime instruments. However, in a somewhat ironic twist, the move towards more market-like mechanisms (with their own built-in accountabilities) actually led to more regulation and even greater emphasis on accountability measures, including additional reporting.

6.1 Tuition

The decade of the 1990s was characterized by major increases in tuition. As provincial governments tightened the fiscal belt, tuition became the major source of income to help offset decreased provincial grants. Part of the story is best summarized in an excerpt from *The Price of Knowledge, 2004*.

> The basic trend in university tuition for full-time students is fairly simple. Nationally during the 1980s, real tuition levels were basically stagnant at about $1,800 (in 2003 real dollars) for both undergraduate and graduate students. In 1990 the situation began to change when the province of Quebec – which had frozen tuition since the 1960s – announced a tuition increase of approximately 130 percent over two years. While Quebec froze its fees again shortly thereafter, tuition in other jurisdictions continued to rise throughout most of the 1990s. Between 1989-90 and 1997-98, undergraduate tuition doubled. Outside Quebec tuition has continued to rise since then, albeit at a more moderate pace.[66]

The Price of Knowledge excerpt captures part of the story but there are at least four additional comments worth considering.

First, as noted in the Quebec example, there are major differences by province. After allowing tuition to increase more or less in line with other provinces for part of the 1990s, Manitoba, Prince Edward Island, and Newfoundland and Labrador, adopted policies of holding the line (PEI.) or reducing tuition. After a bout of partial deregulation in the 1996 – 1999 period, Ontario limited undergraduate tuition increases to 2 percent annually and in the most recent two years (under a new government) imposed a tuition freeze. For much of the period in question, tuition in B.C. was frozen. Beginning in 2002, however, B.C. experienced its own version of "deregulation" which lasted until 2005 when the government imposed a 2 percent ceiling on tuition increases. Alberta, Saskatchewan, Nova Scotia and New Brunswick witnessed steady tuition increases throughout the period, albeit often under a framework established or heavily influenced by government.[67]

---

[66] Junor and Usher, op.cit., p. 117
[67] In Nova Scotia for example, a recent *Memorandum of Understanding* between the Province and the Universities establishes a tuition increase limit of 3.9 percent per year for the period 2005-06 through 2007-08.

Second, the increases in tuition (and subsequent freezes, roll-backs, and imposed increase limits) created an on-going uproar on many campuses through much of the 1990s, resulting in a significant amount of additional effort to establish tuition policies, shepherd policies through governance and develop on-going monitoring and reporting mechanisms. At a time when institutions were already coping with the impact of reductions in provincial operating grants the changes in tuition policy increased administrative workloads significantly; a less than optimal environment for the development and implementation of carefully considered policy.

Third, in many provinces the changes in tuition policy were accompanied by changes in government student assistance – including the move from grant-based schemes to loan-based schemes, changes in eligibility, greater emphasis on institutional aid programs, changes in the administration of loan arrangements and then the reintroduction of some provincial grants or bursaries. Students and institutional aid officers coped with a myriad of changes that seemed to add layers of complexity, often resulting in major information system overhauls. Spending on student assistance increased markedly – in fact student assistance became, by far, the fastest growing expenditure in many institutions.

Finally, in the case of some professional programs (e.g., Medicine, Law, Dentistry and a few others) in some provinces, the increase in tuition was considerably greater than a doubling thus creating added concerns about accessibility but, at the same time, providing new resources that were sufficient, in some instances, to point towards quality enhancement. Interestingly, for those particular programs, recent evidence suggests that accessibility for students from low-income families (defined as students whose parents had no post-secondary qualification) actually improved, apparently as a result of efforts to direct some of the increased tuition revenue to additional student assistance.[68] Often those efforts were the direct result of governance oversight, thus providing a powerful incentive to university administrators to focus attention on access for under-represented groups.[69]

A review of the period since 1990 indicates quite clearly that actually "de-regulating" tuition was in fact more difficult than it might have appeared. Attempts to allow greater freedom in the setting of tuition were accompanied by provincial regulations that were actually quite restrictive. Moreover, specific conditions actually induced behaviours that may have been less than optimal in terms of supporting access and quality. For example, in Ontario the Conservative government's attempt to "deregulate" tuition was accompanied by a requirement to "set-aside" a portion of the increased tuition for student assistance. Coupled with the establishment of ceilings on the amount of provincial student assistance, the set-aside was seen as a way to ensure that institutions contributed to the cost of any student assistance requirements arising from increases in tuition. Within a few years of the establishment of the set-aside other factors came into play. Earmarked funding for increased enrolment in certain programs resulted in increased competition for certain students interested in those programs. The establishment of "enrolment

---

[68] M. Frenette, *The Impact of Tuiton Fees on University Access: Evidence from a Large-Scale Price Deregulation in Professional Programs*, Statistics Canada, September 2005. Frenette also found that the proportion of students from families categorized as middle-educated (parents with post-secondary qualifications, but not graduate or professional degrees) declined and he suggests that may be related to the increased costs and less availability of student assistance. Readers should note the Frenette study is based on a small sample of professional students.

[69] See, for example, *Policy on Student Financial Support*, University of Toronto, 1998

targets" by the province – and the requisite grant funding associated with those targets – added further to the competitive fray. Not surprisingly, a portion of the set-aside monies began to be used to recruit students. Some funds that were ostensibly to be earmarked for 'needs-based assistance' were directed to student recruitment – much of it in the form of non-renewable entrance awards.[70]

6.2. Developments in Degree-granting

Tackling the degree granting monopoly of universities was seen by some governments (Ontario, Alberta, and BC) as critically important for at least two reasons: first to increase the capacity of the post-secondary sector to handle increased demand for degrees; and second to introduce more competition into the post-secondary sector.

A recent article by David Marshall, former President of Nipissing University in Ontario and now President of Mount Royal College in Alberta, chronicles the various strategies adopted by governments across the country to cope with the increased demand. Those strategies included expanding existing universities, creating new universities, creating new post-secondary institutions with degree granting authority (i.e., university colleges), offering and expanding college-university transfer programs, expanding the number of college-university joint programs, and encouraging more off-campus (distance) education.[71] A number of provinces (BC, Alberta, and Ontario) also established frameworks to allow private degree granting institutions and public universities from other jurisdictions the opportunity to offer degree programs.

The establishment of a number of the preceding strategies to help address the enrolment demand added considerable uncertainty and angst to the post-secondary sector. Against a background of government cut-backs, and the pervasiveness of neo-liberal philosophy among some governments, many of the initiatives were interpreted as evidence of government intentions to avoid providing the necessary investment to sustain and expand *existing* universities. The extension of degree granting authority beyond 'traditional' universities (i.e., to colleges, and university-colleges) was seen by some as nothing more than 'mission creep'. The establishment of new designations (i.e., applied degrees) gave rise to a set of issues regarding the appropriateness of the credential and how to treat such credentials (and programs) in assessing transfers and applications to professional programs and graduate schools. Some colleges in some provinces were granted expanded mandates but the funding did not change – neither the funding mechanism nor the funding levels. New mechanisms and processes were required to provide quality assurance at the provincial level, but little was done to address quality assurance at the *national* level.[72]

---

[70] F. Gucciardi, *Recognizing Excellence? Canada's Merit Scholarships*, Canada Millennium Scholarship Foundation, March 2004. p.13
[71] Marshall, D. *Degree Accreditation in Canada*, The Canadian Journal of Higher Education, Vol. XXXIV, No.2 2004
[72] In the absence of a national accreditation body for universities, membership in the Association of Universities and Colleges of Canada (AUCC) is the *de facto* standard. As new institutions and institutions with new degree designation clamoured for AUCC membership, AUCC imposed a moratorium on membership to consider its membership criteria. The question that is now front and centre is whether those 'new' degree designations will be acceptable across the country for admittance to second-entry professional programs and graduate programs.

The regulatory changes in degree-granting were first and foremost intended to address access concerns and specifically the increasing demand for degree credentials. Not surprisingly, the pressure for change was the greatest in Alberta, Ontario and British Columbia – three provinces experiencing strong enrolment demand or where government recognized the need to improve access opportunities.

There are clearly more institutions offering degrees now than there were a few years ago. During the more recent period of relatively rapid expansion those institutions have helped absorb increases in student demand. Moreover, because geographical proximity is a factor that appears to affect participation in post-secondary education,[73] and the choice of whether to pursue a college diploma or university degree, the existence of more institutions should have a positive influence on access to university degree opportunities.

The impact on quality is more difficult to determine. Given the quality assurance processes that individual provinces put in place to review proposals for degree granting, one could argue that the minimum requirements are at least as rigorous as degree requirements at some existing degree granting institutions. This is clearly an area for future research and is dependent on having a quality measurement system that focuses on outputs and outcomes.

Whether the changes in degree granting have 'opened' the post-secondary system to more competition is worthy of more study as well. During a period of expansion, it is unlikely such changes have had a major impact on competition among universities – there are still relatively few 'private' universities and their enrolments are relatively small. However, one might see greater competition among colleges – those that have degree granting programs versus those that do not have such programs. Again, this is an area for future research.

At the same time it is interesting to note that throughout the country a number of provincial governments also moved towards a more unified view of post-secondary education. A number of commissions/reviews/task forces were provided with mandates that included reviews of both universities and colleges. Inevitably the commission or task force would recommend measures to improve co-operation and collaboration between the sectors to improve efficiencies as well as access. In some cases those recommendations resulted in new bodies being established to facilitate co-operation and collaboration. To a sector feeling overburdened trying to service the expanded demands from increased enrolment from traditional sources of demand (i.e., secondary school) and increased research activity, the new bodies simply represented another regulatory agency.

6.3. Accountability

Another major factor that has influenced post-secondary education over the past fifteen years or so is the growing interest in public sector accountability. That particular reality is not confined to the post-secondary sector. All parts of the public sector and broader public sector have been

---

Membership in AUCC is often regarded as an admission criterion for Canadian students applying with a Canadian degree designation.

[73] M. Frenette, *Access to College and University: Does Distance Matter?*, Statistics Canada, June 2003

subject to increased calls for greater accountability and the attendant templates and reporting requirements.

The greater interest in accountability has played out differently by sector and province recognizing the quite different relationships between governments and the institutions and changes over time in the perceived intent and value of accountability initiatives. Initially seen as intrusive and a recipe for government micro-management with a single goal of containing expenditures[74], the value of good accountability frameworks is now generally recognized as an important ingredient in the overall management and operation of post-secondary institutions. Moreover, over time, the emphasis has shifted from a more narrow view of adherence to policies and procedures and financial accountability, to a more comprehensive view of accountability with an onus on multi-year plans[75] and performance measures - often developed jointly (or at least with some consultation) by government and the institutions.

But, it has been a tortuous process. Within the university sector in Ontario, for example, the following table lists the various formal accountability initiatives that occurred since the late 1980s.

Summary of Provincial Accountability Initiatives for Ontario Universities

- 1988 to 1991: Inspection Audits of 3 Universities by Provincial Auditor
- 1991 to 1993: Task Force on University Accountability (Broadhurst Report)
- 1995: Ontario Financial Review Commission
- 1997: Ontario Budget – discussion of Public Sector Accountability Act
- 1999: Report of the Provincial Auditor on University Accountability
- 2000-2001: COU-Ministry Task Force on the Provincial Auditor's Report
- 2001: Public Sector Accountability Act (proposed)
- 2003: Multi-Year Base Funding Accountability Framework (pending)
- 2003/04: Bill 18 Expanding the powers of the Provincial Auditor (value-for-money audits)

Source: Council of Ontario Universities

There are many positive outcomes associated with the increased interest in accountability including better reporting of some information, greater interest in performance measures and performance measurement, and increased curiosity about the factors that influence improvements in performance.[76] There are, however, some outcomes that may have led to unintended

---

[74] For example, Quebec's Bill 198, an *Act respecting the reduction of personnel in public bodies and the accountability of deputy ministers and chief executive officers of public bodies,* called for a 20 percent reduction in management staff and a 12 percent reduction in all other personnel. While the Act was later amended and eventually repealed, in the short-term it focussed attention on expenditure reduction.

[75] Interestingly, the exception to that trend is Quebec where the Charest government jettisoned the multi-year performance contract approach of the former government and now demands annual balanced budgets. See C. Trottier and J. Bernatchez *Higher Education Policy in Québec: A Case Study,* May 2005

[76] In Quebec, for example, another outcome of increased interest in accountability is the requirement for universities to file an annual report to The National Assembly Education Commission and appear before the Commission every three years, an idea that was included in the Rae Report – *Ontario: A Leader in Learning.*

consequences, partly because there are different interpretations of accountability.[77] The availability of more information about the post-secondary sector and performance measures provided a natural attraction for policy makers to try to steer performance improvements – through funding envelopes – without fully understanding the various factors that influence performance at the institutional level. And performance is sometimes regarded as synonymous with quality.

Another outcome was a proliferation of required reporting associated with earmarked government grants and government regulations. Under the banner of accountability, government needed to capture considerably more information to meet its own accountability requirements.[78] In an era of government 'business plans' with goals and objectives, the need to report results – even if those results were viewed as isolated numbers somewhat removed from the core operations of the institution – became paramount. The end result has been a significant increase in reporting.[79]

As noted at the outset, the actual government initiated accountability arrangements differ by province and by sector. This is yet another area worthy of study to catalogue, chronicle and assess the evolving approaches to accountability.

A final outcome of the increased interest in accountability has been a greater involvement of institutional governance in paying attention to risk management and establishing an appropriate institutional accountability framework. For board members who may have questioned the role and effectiveness of governing bodies, the interest in accountability has (or should have) helped focus their attention.

Together the changes in the regulatory environment had a profound impact on colleges and universities in many provinces over the period. When coupled with changes in provincial funding support and changes in the funding mechanisms, colleges and universities seemed to be subjected to an unending series of external 'shocks' – that posed significant challenges to administrators and governors alike – such as making planning extraordinarily difficult – and underscored the power of the government and the tools it could use (funding, policy, regulation) to influence the post-secondary sector.

---

[77] Janice Gross Stein argues there are two distinct kinds of accountability in public institutions: procedural and substantive: "There is accountability about rules and procedures – the way I do things – and accountability about substance – what I do." The former accountability is relatively easy to define and monitor; the latter is much more difficult at least partly because of the multiple and competing accountabilities inherent in colleges and universities (to students, to various 'funders', to the Board of Governors, to departmental colleagues and discipline colleagues inside and outside the institution). *The Unbearable Lightness of Being: Universities as Performers* in Iacobucci and Tuohy, eds., Taking Public Universities Seriously, University of Toronto Press, 2005.

[78] An interesting example was the need for institutional audits of the Ontario Student Assistance Program (OSAP) in light of the Provincial Auditor's review of the OSAP program. It was 'interesting' for three reasons: 1) many of the problems identified by the Provincial Auditor, were, in fact, attributed to the Private Vocational Schools but the mandated audits applied to all institutions in the post-secondary sector; 2) the cost of the audits had to be absorbed by the institution; and 3) the imposed audits underscored the growing power of the Provincial Auditor.

[79] For a listing of reporting requirements in Ontario see Council of Ontario Universities, *Proposed University Accountability Framework*, Appendix B, Submitted by COU to the Post-secondary Review, November 15, 2004

The preceding sections on tuition, degree-granting and accountability have provided a brief review of some of the components of the regulatory environment. There are a number of other areas that deserve attention including: regulations governing the eligibility of enrolments for public support; regulations regarding the portability of provincial student assistance across the country, differential fees for out-of-province students (Quebec), tuition policies for internationals students; and whether international enrolments are 'eligible' for public support. Each of those topics is worthy of examination for such an examination would indicate, yet again, major differences by province and major changes since the early 1990s.

6.4 Changes in Funding Mechanisms and the Regulatory Environment: Impact on Internal Resource Allocation

Before turning to access and quality, it is important to comment on the impact of the preceding funding and regulatory changes on internal resource allocation developments at the institutional level. At any one time a number of the preceding factors were at play, and often all of the factors were influencing institutional decisions in a variety of areas – resource allocation, enrolment levels, program development, student assistance policy, fund-raising priorities, tuition levels and capital investment.

As we have seen previously, the post-secondary environment was subject to enormous pressures over the period in question. For most of the 1990s, universities and colleges were struggling to cope in an environment that appeared, at times, to be unstable and unpredictable with financial constraint and cut-backs as the single constant. As the post-secondary environment began moving from retrenchment to expansion – initially quite selective expansion – the post-secondary financial environment had changed, dramatically. Increases in tuition and changes in tuition policy increased the importance of tuition revenue. Earmarked provincial grants for expansion in certain discipline areas focused attention on enrolment in specific disciplines. Research funds tended to be concentrated in NSERC and CIHR disciplines. Funding differences began to emerge <u>within</u> individual institutions – heavily influenced by external factors but reinforced by changes in internal resource allocation policies and practices.

One of the key characteristics of institutional funding since the 1960s, in some jurisdictions, had been a reliance on 'bloc funding' involving both grants and tuition fees, based on student enrolments. In some provinces different weightings were employed to reflect differences in program costs (i.e., Medicine versus Arts) within an institution but the final product – the operating grant – was intended as a bloc grant to the institution as noted in the following excerpt from the original funding formula proposal for universities in Ontario.

> It cannot be over-emphasized that the formula is designed to produce a reasonably equitable over-all distribution of basic university income. *It is not intended as a pattern for spending.* (emphasis added) The formula weights do not reflect the very important differences in costs among the various subjects within a given program or among course years. These differences are averaged out in the weighting process and not significant for the relatively simple income producing formula proposed.[80]

---

[80] Committee on University Affairs, *A Formula for Operating Grants to Provincially-Assisted Universities in Ontario*, Report to the Ministry of University Affairs, November, 1966.

One of the major changes that occurred on many campuses over the past decade was the more direct linking of income to specific programs. Prior to the mid-1990s there was little difference between tuition for a medical student and tuition for an arts student and tuition levels were essentially controlled by government in most provinces. Once some professional fees were "deregulated" in some provinces, the question naturally arose inside the institution "Who gets the income?" Deans were willing to accept responsibility for differential fees but only if a major part of the incremental income found its way to the Faculty/School where the Dean could demonstrate to the students that the increased tuition income was having a positive impact on the learning environment. Similarly, as governments provided earmarked grants for enrolment expansion in specific programs it was expected that those specific programs would be the recipients of the additional grant income. Again, Deans were prepared to recruit more students in specific programs but only if the provincial grant funding and the associated tuition income (or a portion thereof) found its way into the Faculty/School.

In a very short period of time, internal resource allocation models that had been based on a variety of factors (including history) but often centrally controlled in the President or Provost's Office, began to crumble under *ad hoc* modifications intended to respond to the new funding reality. 'Responsibility Centred Budgeting' and 'Each Tub on Its Own Bottom' became part of the academic administrator's lexicon as did 'haves' and 'have nots'. For the most part institutions are still adjusting to the changed funding environments and still experimenting with appropriate resource allocation policies and processes.

For the 'haves' (certain professional programs and the broadly defined 'sciences') it was soon obvious that earmarked government funding and increased funding from non-government sources were, in fact, resulting in a relatively better learning environment – more faculty, better facilities, more research assistantship funding, etc. In some professional programs increased enrolment was accompanied by an acknowledged increase in the factors that were purported to influence quality.

For the 'have-nots' the fear (and reality) that 'money talks' was finding its way into the somewhat hallowed halls of academe added to the general uproar. Initially, greater concern was expressed about the steering effects of earmarked government funding, contract research, gifts from corporations, foundations and private individuals. But as policies were put in place to administer the various sources of funds, and as the 'expansion' began to impact all parts of the institution, and as individuals began to see the value of the new investments in terms of more faculty, better facilities, better starting salaries and very reasonable compensation increases, some of the angst decreased. The impact of some Faculties/Schools hiring top-notch faculty, and paying them accordingly, seemed to have a salutary effect as the overall condition of the professoriate improved.

Another related factor that deserves comment was the adoption of multi-year planning and budgeting strategies by some institutions. That move, initially by the University of Toronto and now adopted by a number of institutions across the country, helped immeasurably to smooth the ups and downs of government funding and changes in government policies. While many institutions reacted to provincial cut-backs in funding with major down-sizing initiatives driven by a short-sighted fixation on 'balancing the budget'(sometimes mandated by government), a few institutions took a somewhat longer-term view consistent with the longer-term interests and expenditure realities in post-secondary education. While those institutions were not immune to the ups and downs of government actions, they were better able to seize opportunities and weather the worst of a very stormy period.

Finally, it is important to note that colleges and universities were not complete 'innocents' with respect to funding mechanisms and the regulatory environment. In the face of cut-backs in provincial operating grants, many institutions lobbied for more tuition flexibility. Some institutions also lobbied for earmarked grants – both to facilitate compensation negotiations and as a way to pry monies from governments intent on deficit cutting. As noted earlier, the university community 'signed on' to the Federal Innovation Strategy and all that it entailed, including the pressures it brought to bear on the provinces. The 'bottom line': almost any money was better than no money.

Having provided a review of funding and funding mechanisms, and having commented on the three major regulatory developments of the past fifteen years or so, the report now turns to brief reviews of what we know about Access and Quality.

7. Access: What Do We Know?

According to a recent CPRN study by Patrice de Broucker[81]

1. High levels of <u>college</u> attainment result in Canada leading the OECD countries in terms of the proportion of the population with tertiary education. University participation is relatively high but a number of countries rank higher and/or are making faster progress in increasing the proportion of the population with university experience.
2. Young people … from high-income families are two to three times more likely to go to university than young people from low-income families. The proportion of those going to college is more evenly distributed across family-income levels."
3. …while financial considerations do play a role in determining access… they are not the only determinant, nor even the most directly important. Instead, family financial resources blend with parents' education and expectations, geography and institutional capacity to influence everyone's educational pathways from very early on."

De Broucker's thoughtful study provides an added bonus in that it is accompanied by a summary report of a literature review on access to post-secondary education.[82] Readers interested in a review of the various research studies on access are encouraged to refer to the report.

Based on findings presented by Junor/Usher in *The Price of Knowledge 2004* there are a number of other observations that can be made about access. In terms of socio-economic characteristics the report indicates a

> major reduction in educational disparity over the 20 year period under investigation … the participation rate of children from families with family incomes below $25,000 went from just under 9 percent for university and 14 percent for colleges in 1979 to 20 percent and 22 percent respectively, in 1997. The gradual inclusion of lower-income students in post-secondary education and in the university sector in particular over this period is an important success story in Canadian education.[83]

In terms of combined college and university participation rates, the Junor/Usher report indicates that the national participation rate increased from just below 30 percent in 1990 to 35 percent by 2003. *But much of that change occurred in the period prior to the major funding cut-backs in the mid-1990s and after the provinces began investing in expansion.* Capacity, or more correctly lack of capacity, may well account for the relatively flat participation rates that characterized the period from the mid-90s to, roughly, the turn of the century. In most provinces and at both the college and university levels, participation rates were relatively flat.[84] With hindsight that should not be surprising. Institutions across the country "hunkered down" in the mid-1990s and focused

---

[81] De Broucker, P., *Getting There and Staying There: Low-income Students and Post-secondary Education*, Canadian Policy Research Networks, April 2005.
[82] De Broucker, P., and Mortimer, K., *Research Summary Table: Access to PSE*, Canadian Policy Research Networks, March 2005.
[83] Junor and Usher, op.cit., p. 56
[84] Ibid., pp. 50-51

on down-sizing, cut-backs, and coping with a myriad of changes as described previously. Reduced funding affected capacity and provided little room for improving access. As the baby-boom echo reached the post-secondary doorstep beginning in 1998, institutions had difficulty just absorbing the increase in the demographic demand, never mind trying to improve participation rates. The infusion of additional funds over the following few years (provincial, federal and, in some cases, tuition) helped provide the wherewithal to increase capacity.

There were major variations across the country in the level of participation rates with Quebec and Nova Scotia registering the highest participation rates (over 40 percent) and British Columbia and Saskatchewan registering the lowest (below 25 percent). In fact, all of the western provinces register well below the national average.

The preceding data refer to a combined college and university participation. If the figures are disaggregated it is clear that much of the increase in participation rates is actually in the university sector, but again, the results vary by province with Nova Scotia leading the pack (39 percent), and Alberta and British Columbia hovering around 15 percent.[85]

There are many reasons for the differences in participation by province, but, as noted in the following quote from the Junor/Usher report, differences in post-secondary capacity have a marked influence on participation and access:

> … secondary school students from Alberta and British Columbia have much higher literacy scores than their counterparts in Atlantic Canada. … And yet, far more students attend university in the Atlantic provinces than in Alberta and BC. The main reason? Smaller university capacity in the west and lower academic standards in the east … Between 20-25 percent of the entering university class in the Atlantic provinces have average secondary school marks below 75 percent while the corresponding figure in BC is only 2 percent.[86]

Capacity, it seems, not only affects the changes in participation rates over time but also helps explain provincial differences.[87]

In terms of meeting current enrolment *demand*, for university education a report prepared for the Millennium Foundation concluded that:

> In most provinces it appears that applicant demand from secondary school/CEGEP has been met as first year enrolment increases are keeping pace with the demand (applicants). However, in British Columbia, it is clear, over the period in question, that the increase in applicant demand from secondary school graduates is not being met. Moreover, in Alberta the most recent experience (fall 2003) represents a

---

[85] The participation rate used by Junor/Usher was based on full-time enrolment and 19-22 year-olds in Ontario and Quebec, and 18-21 year-olds elsewhere.
[86] Educational Policy Institute, "The Price of Knowledge, Behind the Headlines", in *epicentre*, Fall 2004
[87] Interestingly a calculation of participation rates using the 18-24 year-old age group and the Statistics Canada Labour Force Survey data (special tabulations) as reported in a *Profile of Alberta's Advanced Education System*, shows somewhat different participation rates with Newfoundland leading the university sector and BC well over 20 percent.

departure from the previous year in that applicant demand appears to have outpaced the increase in the number of available spaces – at least at the University of Alberta. Having experienced one of the highest growth rates in the 18-19 year old population in the country the Alberta situation bears close monitoring.[88]

Increased participation rates, improvements in the socio-economic profile of post-secondary students, and evidence that applicants are being accommodated are results that indicate an overall improvement in access over the past fifteen years. Yet, as noted earlier by de Broucker, other countries are improving their participation rates as well – especially at the university level. Moreover, it is not at all clear that students are actually getting access to the programs and institutions of their first choice, another area that deserves further study.

There is also increasing interest in 'reaching out' to under-represented groups and enhancing access opportunities. References to improving access for under-represented groups are liberally sprinkled throughout a number of recent Commission studies across the country and provincial governments appear to have picked up the message. In Ontario, for example, the Post-secondary Review explicitly recognized the importance of improving access for aboriginals, francophone, the disabled and "Young people who would be the first generation in their family to attend a college or university."[89] The recent Throne Speech from the Ontario Government made explicit reference to the First Generation Plan "designed to help those students striving to become the first in their families to seek a post-secondary education."[90]

Improving access further requires a better understanding of the factors that are influencing current levels of access. We have seen that capacity constraints have a measured impact on access. At the same time, as reported by de Broucker and in the Junor/Usher study, there are other factors that have been noted as major barriers to access.

> In increasing order of importance, the three kinds of barriers (to access and participation) are academic, financial and informational/motivational.[91]

In the case of *academic* barriers, the authors of *The Price of Knowledge 2004* conclude that:

> They are a much more important deterrent for students attempting to enter universities (which have selective application procedures).... Since academic marks are positively correlated to socio-economic background, an increase in selectivity is bound to have a greater negative effect on youth from low-income backgrounds ....[92]

Junor and Usher recognize the importance of *financial* barriers but also note the complexity associated with the topic:

---

[88] Snowdon, K., *Applicant Data in Canada: Another Perspective on Access*, Canada Millennium Scholarship Foundation, December 2004, p. i .
[89] Hon. Bob Rae, op.cit., p.66
[90] Honourable J.K. Bartleman, *Strengthening Ontario's Economic Advantage*, Government of Ontario, October 12, 2005, p.9
[91] Junor and Usher, op.cit., p.91
[92] Ibid., p.91

While financial barriers are often considered to be of a single type, there are in fact three different kinds: *price constraints* (i.e., the price of education is considered too high for the expected return), *cash constraints* (i.e., the price of education is considered reasonable, but the individual does not have the financial wherewithal to attend) and *debt aversion* (i.e., the price is reasonable and sufficient funding available, but the individual is unwilling to borrow).[93]

Finally, in commenting on *motivational/informational* barriers – the authors of the same report suggest that:

About half of all youth who do not pursue post-secondary studies say they are not interested in doing so. These youth appear to come predominantly from lower-income backgrounds. They may be uninterested in higher education in part because of the extremely erroneous information lower-income Canadians appear to have regarding the costs and benefits of post-secondary studies.[94]

What is to be done? De Broucker, calls for a five part approach to improving access: Early intervention; more career-oriented options; information and counselling; providing adequate public investment to ensure tuition is kept reasonable; and greater reliance on needs based grant assistance for low-income students. To those measures one should add the importance of providing more post-secondary spaces. There is little sense in adopting a host of measures to improve access if, in fact, colleges and universities are 'running out of room'.

To their credit, the provinces with the lowest participation rates and burgeoning demand appear to recognize the underlying importance of adding capacity. Recent announcements in Alberta and British Columbia suggest those governments clearly recognize the need to further expand capacity and improve access opportunities with Alberta committed to adding 15,000 new post-secondary spaces over the next three years and BC committed to an additional 25,0000 spaces.

Alberta Budget 2005 highlights:

- A 30 percent increase in overall funding for Advanced Education over the next three years.
- An 18 percent increase over three years in base operating grants for post-secondary institutions, six percent per year.
- A $5.7-million increase in 2005-06 for apprenticeship training.
- An 11.7 percent increase in 2005-06 for scholarships, bursaries, and grants.
- Coverage of 2005-06 tuition increases, saving students $43-million.
- $469 million in post-secondary capital projects over the next three years.
- A $250-million initial payment from surplus funds to kick-start the $3-billion Access to the Future endowment.[95]

---

[93] Ibid., p.91
[94] The latter point is explored in more detail in *A Little Knowledge is a Dangerous Thing: How Perceptions of Costs and Benefits Affect Access to Education*, Educational Policy Institute, 2005
[95] http://www.advancededucation.gov.ab.ca/department/budget/2005/

British Columbia

> Between now and 2010, we'll be adding 25,000 new student spaces at colleges, universities and institutes across the province. Our goal is to ensure that students who get a B or better in high school will have the opportunity to go to university closer to home, and to build their futures in a province that is second to none.[96]

In 2005 Ontario also embarked on a major public investment to improve access and quality.

> This Budget announces the McGuinty government's action plan for colleges, universities and training, highlighted by a $6.2 billion cumulative investment by 2009-10. This investment includes an additional $683 million in 2005-06, rising to $1.6 billion by 2009-10. This historic, multi-year investment in post-secondary education – the largest in 40 years – would represent a 39 percent increase compared to the 2004-05 funding base. With the Reaching Higher investments, the people of Ontario will see improved access and quality in post-secondary education, better facilities, and post-secondary institutions will be held accountable for accomplishing these objectives.[97]

As noted earlier in this paper, provincial differences in the post-secondary demographic pose differing challenges. Given the projected increase in the number of 18-19 year olds in B.C., Alberta and Ontario, it should not be surprising that it is those three provinces that have announced major investments to cope with increased and expected increases in demand. But the interest in increasing access (and participation rates) goes beyond simply meeting demographic challenges because, as noted in the Honourable Bob Rae's report *Ontario: A Leader in Learning*, " the new economy demands it, the number of people attending will *need* to rise substantially in the years ahead."[98] (*emphasis added*)

Heightened interest in improving access bodes well for the Canadian post-secondary sector but it is imperative that the 'interest' is accompanied by adequate resources. And the definition of 'adequate' resources extends beyond the average student funding levels associated with post-secondary investments to date. As greater attempts are made to improve access for underrepresented groups it should come as no surprise that those students will require higher than average levels of support services.[99]

---

[96] Ministry of Advanced Education, *New Post-Secondary Student Spaces to Date*, Ministry website, July 27, 2005
[97] Ministry of Finance, *2005 Ontario Budget, Backgrounder, Reaching Higher: the McGuinty Government Plan for Post-secondary Education*, May 11, 2005
[98] Hon. Bob Rae, op.cit., p.7
[99] Findings from the U.K. suggest that the recruitment and retention of non-traditional students costs approximately 30 percent more than 'traditional' students. (See Universities UK, Achieving our Vision, 2004 Spending Review Submission for England and Northern Ireland)

8. Quality: What Do We Know?

> ... the problem is that while everybody wants a "quality" post-secondary education system, institutions, governments and other stakeholders do not always agree at the even more fundamental level of how quality should be defined.[100]

The preceding quote from a recent study about measuring 'quality', aptly sums up the current state of what we know about quality in higher education; everybody wants "it" but it is not clear exactly what "it" is.

In a paper delivered to the Higher Education in Canada Conference in early 2004, the Chair of the Council of Ontario Universities Quality and Financing Task Force suggested that quality in a university setting was defined on the basis of "these commonly-accepted indicators";[101]

- low faculty/student ratios
- a wide choice of courses and programs
- well-equipped, up-to-date laboratories and classrooms
- well stocked libraries that make use of leading edge technology
- highly qualified faculty members
- adequate support staff and services, and
- well-maintained facilities

It is not clear whether those "indicators" are, in fact, commonly accepted (except perhaps by university presidents). However, it is clear that this specific definition of quality is framed around *resources* and *inputs* rather than educational processes or outputs and outcomes. Based on a review of resource comparisons over time and with other jurisdictions, much of the COU analyses reinforce the notion that quality has declined in absolute terms and relative terms. Student to faculty ratios have increased as faculty numbers have not kept pace with changes in enrolment, leading to larger class sizes and less student/faculty interaction. Further, we know faculty are having to spend more time on research thus the change in student to faculty ratios is under-reporting the real situation on many campuses. Libraries are struggling trying to keep up with the demands of a digital age, the explosion in new knowledge, and the price escalation of journals and monographs. Facilities have deteriorated in the face of funding constraints and deferred maintenance is now regarded as a major problem on many campuses. In Ontario, for example, the deferred maintenance backlog is estimated at $1.8 billion – and is considered serious enough to garner a recommendation from the Post-secondary Review for "up to $200 million of critical repair work in each of the next three years." (p.88) There is a reasonably clear indication that the quantity of the inputs (expressed on a per student basis) has diminished. But whether that reality translates directly into diminished quality is more difficult to discern.

One of the reasons it is difficult to discern is that, arguably, the quality of the faculty has improved. Faculty hired in the past fifteen years often have a track record of research publication and teaching experience before they land their first tenure-track appointment. To the extent that

---

[100] Finnie, R. and Usher A., *Measuring the Quality of Post-secondary Education: Concepts, Current Practices and a Strategic Plan*, Canadian Policy Research Networks, April 2005 p.1
[101] George, P., "Financing Quality in Ontario Universities", in C. Beach et al., *Higher Education in Canada*, p.559

the quality of faculty is a critical input into the overall assessment of higher education quality one might conclude that some aspects of quality may have actually improved. Whether improvements in one area are sufficient to offset deterioration in another area (i.e., the actual number of faculty per student) is difficult to determine by solely looking at inputs.

There are two[102] other factors that make one pause when considering the rather simple resource inputs perspective on quality. First the 1990s were marked by considerable investments in teaching effectiveness. Virtually every college and university now has a Centre that provides workshops and support for curriculum development, effective teaching practices, incorporating technology into the classroom and a host of related activities. How those investments have affected 'quality' is beyond the scope of this paper but one might speculate that the investments have had a positive impact and helped offset some of the more negative aspects associated with reduced resource inputs.

Second, quality assurance practices are considerably more common now than they were in 1990. To the extent that individual institutions and various third-party bodies are actively engaged in program reviews, one could argue that greater attention is being paid to 'quality' and the factors that influence quality. The very fact that there are quality assurance processes in place certainly suggests the existence of minimum quality standards or expectations of quality and, perhaps more importantly, interest in improving quality.

In *The Evidence for Quality*,[103] the authors note that "Americans have fashioned a complex pattern of practices in our search for quality. Among those are the following:

- Accreditation: the test of goal achievement and improvement
- Rankings and ratings: the test of reputation
- Outcomes: the test of results
- Licensure: the test of professional standards
- Program reviews: the test of peer review
- Follow-up studies: the test of client satisfaction"

The American experience is instructive because it acknowledges the complexities associated with defining quality by utilizing a variety of measures that, taken as whole, provide a more comprehensive assessment of quality.

In Canada the existence of rankings and licensure requirements, program reviews and various indicators of satisfaction should provide, or could provide, a set of different perspectives on quality. But to this point there has been no systematic evaluation of those various potential sources of information. This an area that deserves further research.

Quality is clearly of increasing interest to governments and the post-secondary sector alike. And it is clear that more effort is required to arrive at appropriate definitions of quality. To that end, the Finnie and Usher report on measuring quality provides an example of a definition that

---

[102] There is likely a third factor as well: the infusion of new research monies but a full examination of the impact on 'quality' is beyond the scope of this paper.
[103] Bogue, E.G. and Saunders, R.L., *The Evidence for Quality*, Jossey-Bass, San Francisco, 1992 p.22

focuses on "the value-added of the educational experience" (p.iii). This more student-focused definition of quality is explained in the following manner:

> The conceptual framework is simple, capturing the PSE experience as a story of inputs and outputs whose narrative flows like this:
> • *Beginning Characteristics* – the characteristics and abilities of incoming students that affect the quality of their educational experience and the outcomes.
> • *Learning Inputs* – the institutional financial resources, material inputs and the organization of those resources which thus comprise the determinants and characteristics of individuals' learning experiences; all are at least potentially controllable and thus amenable to change, improvement, and policy initiatives at various levels.
> • *Learning Outputs* – the "skill sets" or any other attributes of graduates arising from their educational experiences that help determine final outcomes.
> • *Final Outcomes* – the more specific "ultimate ends" to which the educational system may contribute – everything from employment, income and job satisfaction, to civic participation and continued education.

The emphasis on value-added has been explored by others. Twenty years ago Alexander Astin, noted

> "the most excellent institutions are, in this view, those that have the greatest impact – add the most value, as economists would say – on the student's knowledge and personal development and on the faculty member's scholarly and pedagogical ability and productivity.[104]

In Astin's case he focused on both students *and* faculty while Finnie and Usher make it clear that their focus is "primarily on the quality of the education provided by the universities to its students..."[105]

In *How College Affects Student, Volume 2: A Third Decade of Research,* Pascarella and Terezini note that

> ... with some notable exceptions, the weight of evidence from the 1990's casts considerable doubt on the premise that the substantial structural, resources, and qualitative differences among post-secondary institutions produce correspondingly large differences in net educational effects on students. Rather the great majority of post-secondary institutions appear to have surprisingly similar net impacts on student growth, although the "start" and "end" points for students differs across the institutions."[106]

---

[104] Astin, A., *Achieving Educational Excellence: A Critical Assessment of Priorities and Practices in Higher Education*, San Francisco: Jossey-Bass 1985, p.361) quoted in Bogue and Saunders, Ibid., p.12.
[105] Finnie R., and Usher A., Op.cit., p.3
[106] Pascarella, E. and Terezini, P., *How College Affects Students:, Volume 2: A Third Decade of Research*, Jossey-Bass, 2005 p. 590

If quality is determined by assessing changes (value-added) in what Pascarella and Terenzini call 'student growth' (e.g., cognitive skills, attitudes and values, development of verbal, quantitative and subject matter competence, educational attainment etc.) then it follows that the factors influencing those changes in student growth are key to understanding what constitutes a quality experience. The authors sum up the key factors as follows:

> ...the impact of college is largely determined by individual effort and involvement in the academic, interpersonal and extracurricular offerings on campus.[107]

Individual effort and involvement, or what is often called 'student engagement', seems to be the key factor influencing a quality learning experience as defined by Pascarella and Terenzini. Measuring student engagement and understanding those factors that influence student engagement are the focus of the National Survey on Student Engagement (NSSE) – the "leading authoritative voice dedicated to improving undergraduate education, enhancing student success, and promoting collegiate quality."[108]

Canadian universities and colleges are just beginning to implement NSSE (or variations thereof) and preliminary results suggest the level of engagement is somewhat less in Canadian institutions than in the United States. To the extent that NSSE helps improve 'quality' by more sharply highlighting the factors that influence a quality learning environment, and to the extent that Canadian colleges and universities use those findings to influence the many and varied components of the 'learning environment' the NSSE exercise will add considerably to the dearth of good, reliable, quantitative and qualitative information about higher education quality.

NSSE, by itself, however will not provide a definitive answer to the value-added definition of quality because it does not provide a quantitative assessment of learning or improvements in the skill sets acquired through the learning process. To move in that direction requires a more comprehensive collection of information as detailed in the Finnie/Usher proposal noted earlier. Further, it needs to be reiterated that the 'value-added' definition is but one definition of quality.

To illustrate the latter point, the current review of post-secondary education in Alberta offers the following commentary about defining quality.[109]

> In terms of quality within an advanced education environment, quality is not a self-evident or universally accepted term. It is multi-dimensional and means different things to different stakeholders. This is not to say that an overall judgment of what defines quality cannot be made. For example, many of Alberta Advanced Education's performance measures and indicators (refer to Section 2.4) have been selected because they are considered to be measurements of system quality. These measures indicate and define the dimension of quality currently used by Alberta Advanced Education. Similarly, other jurisdictions have defined

---

[107] Ibid., p. 602
[108] National Survey on Student Engagement, *Viewpoint 2004*, http://www.indiana.edu/~nsse/2004_annual_report/pdf/2004_viewpoint.pdf
[109] Alberta Advanced Education, *Quality in Alberta's Advanced Education system*, July 2005 pp. 2-3. For yet another view of 'quality' see *"What we Heard" A Report of Consultations on Public Post-Secondary Education in Newfoundland and Labrador*, December 2004 p.17

quality from their unique perspective and constructed performance measures to assess dimensional levels of quality preferred for their situation. The same can be said for all advanced education stakeholders, whether this means a learner, a taxpayer or a member of society. Each stakeholder has their own unique set of indicators that define dimensions of quality relevant to their situation. In this light, and for the purposes of this discussion document, a quality advanced education system is defined as one where: *The advanced education system meets the needs of learners, society and the economy.*

The preceding review of 'what we know about quality' suggests there are differing conceptions of quality and that reality adds to the difficulty in attempting to develop standard measures of quality. Moreover, it is evident that, despite the various measures that have been developed to date, there are major information gaps and shortcomings that need to be addressed if we are to better understand and measure 'quality'.

In the face of increased calls for greater accountability, increased interest by Boards of Governors in emphasizing planning and monitoring attainment of objectives, increased interest in private sector funding, increased efforts to lobby government for additional funding, increased reviews of academic programs, and the advent of 'rankings' such as Maclean's, institutions have paid greater attention to 'measuring' things over the past fifteen years. Whether they are the *right* things is the subject of much debate and beyond the scope of this report. What is clear, however, is that since the early 90s there has been a significant increase in the amount of data that purports to measure 'performance' which in turn is sometimes regarded as 'quality'. To the extent those exercises have been used to influence funding, policies, programs, and new initiatives aimed at 'improving the quality of education' one could argue the efforts should be seen as a positive development.

The need to better define quality, and the factors influencing quality, is readily apparent. But it is useful to be reminded of the pitfalls of being swept up into thinking of quality solely as a measurement exercise. "Not everything that can be counted counts; and not everything that counts can be counted."[110] On the other hand, "Nothing exists until it is measured."[111]

I leave the final words on this topic to the late David Smith.

> How does one determine the presence of quality? Most university presidents will be pleased to tell willing (and even unwilling) listeners about the superb quality of their institutions. Trustworthy as such people usually are, their assertions do not fully satisfy everyone, since quality might be simple to define but it is extraordinarily difficult, if not impossible, to measure objectively.[112]

---

[110] David C. Smith *"How will I know if there is quality?"* Report on Quality Indicators and Quality Enhancement in Universities: Issues and Experiences, Council of Ontario Universities, March 2000. p.1

[111] Attributed to Niels Bohr, Nobel Laureate in D.J. Johnston, *Statistics, knowledge and progress*, OECD Observer, No.246-247 December 2004-January 2005.

[112] David C. Smith, op.cit., p.7

Smith's recommendations on improving quality focused on the important roles of institutions themselves paying attention to quality assessment and quality assurance. He also acknowledged the need for better information about quality and quality assessments. But the final recommendation in his report summed up his belief in the factors that would have the greatest impact on quality.

> Primary emphasis should be placed on a strong competitive and collaborative environment with resources comparable to those in competing university sectors. This environment will be the most powerful influence on quality.[113]

---

[113] David C. Smith, ibid., pp.4-5

9. Assessment of Funding Levels and Incentive Structures

Previous sections of this report indicated that:

  a) total funding, from all sources and for all purposes reached an all-time high of an estimated $27.7 billion from an early 1990s level of about $16.3 billion;
  b) once inflation and reporting changes are taken into account, the increase falls to about $6 billion or approximately 30 percent;
  c) once increased enrolment is taken into account, per student funding for colleges and universities in 6 of 10 provinces is below 1992-93 levels;
  d) an expanded research mandate has resulted in additional cost pressures that further erode the level of per student funding;
  e) because of restrictions on the use of some of the monies, the actual increase for core operating requirements is lessened further;
  e) there have been significant shifts in funding sources over time with considerably greater emphasis on tuition, more emphasis on private funding (i.e., donations, private contracts) and considerably less emphasis on provincial grants;
  f) federal research funding and research funding in general, increased markedly since the mid-90s; and
  g) revenue diversification resulted in some unexpected consequences for institutions and governments.

Against that funding background:

  a) allocation mechanisms at both the provincial and federal levels have generally become more complicated and are being used to 'steer' results;
  b) the regulatory environment has become increasingly complicated, especially in areas where government has attempted to introduce more competition and market principles;
  c) heightened interest in accountability led to increased audit requirements and additional reporting with an emphasis on compliance rather than outcomes;
  d) in some cases the federal and provincial funding is, in fact, 'working at cross-purposes';
  e) there is a definite need to restore 'trust' between the various partners responsible for post-secondary education;
  f) access has increased – though there is room for improvement and much of the increase has been the direct result of governments more recently recognizing the importance of increasing capacity;
  g) concerns about 'quality' are beginning to resonate with provincial governments even though there are many different views of 'quality'.

Throughout much of the 1990s many provincial governments simply reduced funding to the post-secondary sector and attempted various restructurings to try to improve efficiencies. Cutbacks in federal funding were the culprit but a wave of neo-liberal philosophy helped provide a framework for redefining government's role, its funding commitment and the 'rules of the game'. Reliance on the 'market' translated into a series of measures aimed, supposedly, at increasing competition which, in turn, would lead to improvements in efficiency, productivity and performance. As the federal government reinvested in higher education it used a number of

funding mechanisms that fit nicely into the neo-liberal philosophy; competitions for funds, matching contributions to meet the test of the 'market', and transfers to individuals.
In terms of the impact on access and quality, a number of observations are warranted beginning with access.

First, in a number of provinces the downturn in provincial grant funding led to reductions or no further increases in enrolment (in the period 1994 to 1997). It is likely that enrolments would have decreased further in some provinces but tuition increases helped maintain capacity. Participation rates essentially were flat.

Second, it appears that in the period 1997 to about 2000 there was little change in participation rates despite increased enrolment growth. In the absence of inflationary funding increases in core operating grants, taking more students became the default action but the increase was simply reflecting the increased demographic. In the process the absolute number of students increased and the diversity of the student body increased as well.

Third, an interesting result of the situations described above, is the tendency, at the margin, to focus limited resources on the greatest return to the institution. Accordingly, in the face of strong demand from 'traditional' sources of university and college students (secondary school) there was little incentive to expand attempts to recruit from under-represented groups, especially if that involved added operating costs.

Fourth, the strategy of relying solely on tuition income to finance access was generally short-lived in most provinces and especially in provinces facing increased demand. The advent of earmarked grants for enrolment increases in targeted areas was, in some provinces relatively short-lived as well in the face of significant increases in student demand. To actually move the participation rate required an investment (or at the very least a signal from government) to increase physical and operating capacity. Ultimately, in the three provinces facing the greatest increases in enrolment demand – B.C., Alberta, and Ontario – significant additional public resources were required to help address the demand for greater access.

Fifth, since 2000 there appears to have been actual increases in access – that is enrolment has outpaced the increase in the 'baby-boom echo' cohort.

Sixth, if provincial governments had recognized the need for greater public investment[114] earlier and provided the required funding to increase capacity there is little question that access – in terms of absolute numbers and participation rates – would have improved further.

Finally, it is worth noting that during the period from about 1993 to 1999, in Ontario, the college and university sectors experienced rather different enrolment patterns. Enrolments in the

---

[114] In fact it is unclear exactly how much greater public investment would have been required. Just because prospective students did not attend a college or university, does not mean they were no longer affecting public finances. For example, students may have stayed in secondary school longer or opted for apprenticeship programs or ended-up on social assistance. In cases where a province may have argued it could not afford to expand access to universities, for example, it may actually have been spending public money on those prospective students in any case. The rather Byzantine nature of public finance budget processes and policies makes it difficult for policy makers to assess the full financial impact of their decisions.

university sector actually declined a bit before moving upwards in 1999. Colleges actually grew during the period by about 20,000 students. Both sectors experienced roughly the same cut in provincial grants. Why the difference? One plausible explanation is the difference in the funding mechanism used to distribute the provincial grant. In the universities case, the funding mechanism provided no funding incentive to grow – that is, an institution's share of provincial operating grants would remain the same as long as its enrolment stayed within + or – 3 percent of what was called the 'corridor mid-point'. Other than tuition income there was no additional income associated with taking additional students above existing levels. As governments (first the NDP, then the Conservatives) reduced the actual level of operating grant over the period, universities began reducing faculty and staff (capacity). Not surprisingly, enrolments levelled off and in some cases declined a bit. The more draconian cuts of the Conservatives (1996) were offset to some extent by increased tuition that helped maintain capacity levels.

In the case of the Colleges, the funding mechanism was based on a three-year moving average of enrolments. Accordingly, an institution could, in fact, garner more of the provincial operating grant 'pie' if its enrolment increased. As the size of the 'pie' decreased, overall college enrolment increased as individual colleges attempted to garner a bigger share. That behaviour, in turn, induced other colleges to try to protect their existing share – and the only way to do that was to take more students. There may well have been other reasons for the different enrolment patterns between Ontario colleges and universities but the difference in provincial grant allocation mechanisms certainly appears to have been one of the factors. Assuming the colleges did not have excess capacity at the outset, the question arises as to how the colleges managed to accommodate such a large increase in enrolment with considerably fewer resources. Was the expansion focused in low-cost programs? How did such an expansion affect the quality of the learning environment? Those questions are beyond the scope of this report but deserve further review.

Turning to an assessment of the impact on quality – at least as defined by the quantity of inputs into the undergraduate learning environment – it appears that quality deteriorated for much of the period and manifested itself in a number of ways: less student to faculty interaction, larger classes, fewer opportunities for major writing assignments, greater use of multiple choice exams, less breadth in course offerings, and deteriorating physical facilities. The number of university full-time faculty dropped from a level of 32,900 in the early 1990s to 29,600 by 1998[115] and is only now getting back to the levels of the early 1990s even though enrolment has increased markedly. As research activity increased, faculty found themselves with less time for student interaction. Increased research activity led to increased pressure and demands on institutional services and facilities that were already strapped from cut-backs in provincial funding. Despite positive investments in academic development centres and quality assurance processes, and despite the apparent improvement in the quality of new faculty hires, the overall assessment is that the quality of the undergraduate learning experience, in particular, deteriorated through the 1990s and into the early years of the 21st century. But, it is largely a subjective assessment.

With respect to research, specifically, the infusion of new monies into those areas has helped improve the quantity of research and the quality of research *infrastructure*. Trying to assess the impact on the quality of research is far beyond the scope of this paper although it clearly bears

---

[115] Statistics Canada, Full-time University Teachers in Canada, CAUT Almanac and AUCC estimates.

examination.[116] Similarly we know little about the impact of the research investments on graduate education. It is possible that in the last few years the quality of graduate education – especially in the sciences, applied sciences, and life sciences – has improved because of the significant increase in research investment. Again, this is an area worthy of further investigation.

There is one further observation that can be made about the many changes in the funding and regulatory environments that occurred in the first part of the period under review. Increased workloads, a deteriorating physical environment, earmarked funding that ignored the importance of core operations, student unrest about tuition increases and rising debt levels, all contributed to increased interest in collective action on many campuses. The result, in some cases, was a move to unionization on some campuses and a considerable increase in the amount of labour disruption. How those developments affected quality and access is difficult to determine but they contributed to the general uproar that seemed to characterize a major part of the 1990s.

So, what lessons are to be learned?

---

[116] For one early assessment of that topic see J. Chant and W. Gibson, *Quantity or Quality? Research at Canadian Universities*, in D. Laidler, ed., Renovating the Ivory Tower: Canadian Universities and the Knowledge Economy, C.D. Howe Institute, April 2002.

10. Conclusions: Key Considerations in Improving Quality and Access

- What are you trying to do? (goals)
- What do you need to get there? (strategies, tools, resources) and
- How would you know that you are making progress? (indicators, public reporting, accountability).

The preceding 'bullet points' act as a framework for setting out some key considerations in improving access and quality in higher education. The first point is relatively straightforward – what are you trying to do? If a quality and accessible post-secondary system is the goal then government(s) must articulate that goal – in consultation and partnership with the institutions that will have the responsibility for making it happen. Provincial circumstances and philosophy differ and one might expect the interpretation of 'what are you trying to do?' will differ as well. Finnie/Usher use the term *Final outcomes* to capture the idea of quality goals and they recognize that those outcomes will range from

> traditional measures as employment rates and incomes, but also any other outcome deemed to be important to individuals and society such as job satisfaction, an appreciation of the finer things in life, "being a good citizen", or continued participation in lifelong learning.

Individual institutions should emphasize different aspects of those quality outcomes and similarly one would expect individual provinces to emphasize different aspects as well.

Similarly, differences should be expected when trying to translate provincial access goals to the institutional level. Some institutions are better suited to develop and deliver outreach programs for under-represented groups, while others are more suited to meeting the needs of more traditional students. Some may place additional emphasis on improved retention and preparation for access to second-degree programs, while others may have a comparative advantage in attracting international students.[117] There are no templates for quality and access, nor should there be.

Regardless of how the goals of access and quality are defined it is imperative that governments recognize the expanded mandates of colleges and universities. The expectations for universities and colleges are considerably different in 2005 than they were in 1990. From teaching and learning and appealing to community interests and needs, the university sector is now also seen as *the* major player in innovation and research, and the sector as a whole (colleges and universities) is a key player in economic development and prosperity – locally, regionally and nationally.

Further, the *process* for developing and defining goals is of key importance and must be characterized by consultation and transparency and preferably lead to a result that is 'owned' by

---

[117] As noted previously government policy as it relates to international students has not been examined in this report. However, suffice it to say that provincial policies differ, and have changed over time, with respect to whether an institution receives operating grants for international students, and with respect to tuition policy.

government and the institutions. A pervasive lack of trust between the various partners responsible for post-secondary education and research characterized a major part of the period under review and was simply not conducive to addressing access and quality concerns.

In the case of the second bullet point, there are several considerations. First, adequate resources must be available – from somewhere.

> The funding of universities must provide them with the necessary resources to carry out their mission of teaching and research by enabling them to attain their objectives of excellence that they have set for themselves and that are expected of them.[118]

Government has an obligation to state what its investment will be, and to provide direction on how it expects any funding shortfalls to be met (i.e., tuition policy). There is no prescription for the 'right' amount of government funding or the appropriate level of government subsidy: provincial circumstances and philosophy differ. But each government has an obligation to be clear about the funding level it is prepared to commit, and clear about what is expected for the investment.

Adequate funding levels compensate for a host of institutional differences that would otherwise invite special cases to be made and separate earmarked funds to be established.

There are ways to determine "adequate funding levels" including, as was noted earlier, referencing competing university (and college) sectors. Entities like the Institute for Competitiveness AND Prosperity have spent considerable time and effort establishing reasonably reliable jurisdictional comparisons. More could be done. Alternatively, efforts could be made to focus on specific inputs that would lead to improvements in the learning environment. For example, how many faculty are required to reduce the student/faculty ratio by a certain percentage or to a targeted level? There is, of course, considerable danger in being overly prescriptive but given the limited number of major cost drivers in higher education, the development of a relatively simple resource model to churn out an estimate of "adequate funding" is certainly possible.

Second, once adequate funding levels are established, a process for annual adjustments could be established based on activity change (enrolment, research), and normal cost pressures, with due regard for changes in the provincial (and federal) fiscal situation. To the extent that higher education is seen as a driver of economic growth, perhaps greater attention should be paid to linking the public investment in higher education to economic growth (GDP) with appropriate averaging to recognize economic cycles.

Third, at the margin, definitions of "adequate funding" will become a flashpoint. Universities and colleges will constantly demand additional resources to match their own aspirations. Rae noted that reality in his review of the situation in Ontario and he pointed to the importance of allowing institutions latitude in setting tuition levels as a key instrument to improving quality and

---

[118] Government of Quebec, *Parliamentary Committee on Education for the Quality, Accessibility and Funding of Universities*, 2003, p.30

differentiation. If government is unwilling to allow greater institutional flexibility in tuition setting, it should recognize the need to encourage increases in other sources of income (i.e., private giving). Otherwise, there will be a constant clamour to provide special grants in recognition of the unique circumstances that virtually every college and university can, and will, claim.

Fourth, for the reasons noted above, it is important to create a climate where private giving and institutional entrepreneurial activity is clearly seen as providing the 'margin of excellence' and a funding source for differentiation and diversification. As those funds have disappeared into general revenues to compensate for reductions in provincial government funding or been diverted to 'matching' programs devised by governments, institutions have lost some of the ability to differentiate themselves and invest in areas that have the capability of moving toward national and international stature.

Fifth, adopt a multi-year perspective. Universities and colleges need predictable and relatively stable levels of funding. The hiring of new professors, the admission of a student, the development and implementation of new programs are multi-year commitments. It is heartening to see that a number of provinces (B.C., Alberta, Ontario, Newfoundland, Nova Scotia) have, in fact, recognized the value of multi-year arrangements and are increasingly prepared to make a multi-year funding commitment. There are considerable efficiencies to be gained from such an approach.

Sixth, keep the funding mechanism(s) few and simple. The more simple a funding mechanism, the easier it is for all the stakeholders to understand the implications of their actions. Moreover, while the funding mechanism should be linked to changes in activity (e.g., enrolment) there should be some buffer to allow for year-over-year changes without triggering major changes in provincial grant funding. The use of such a buffer is entirely consistent with the concept of stability and predictability.

Finally, how would you know you are making progress? There are a host of accountability frameworks that emerged during the period from 1990 to the present. A tendency to use earmarked funds and specific indicators of progress has evolved, in some provinces, to a more expansive accountability framework that recognizes the complexities of post-secondary institutions and the multiplicity of goals associated with a college or university. In those cases, less emphasis is placed on using "performance indicators" to allocate funds than on what might be termed "performance reporting"[119] to monitor progress towards goals. Service contracts, performance contracts, business plans, and multi-year plans are all terms that encompass the basic ideas associated with setting goals, determining the required resources and strategies and providing evidence of progress towards the goals.[120]

Regardless of the specific accountability framework, post-secondary governance bodies must be involved and engaged. There are few things more powerful than a well-informed, engaged Board of Governors with a mandate. To the extent that improving access and quality become a focus of

---

[119] See Burke, J.C. *Achieving Accountability in Higher Education*, Jossey-Bass 2005
[120] Such an approach – regardless of its moniker – is entirely consistent with the Finnie/Usher suggestion of having institutions establish their own mechanism for defining and monitoring quality.

governance, steps will be taken to ensure there is demonstrable progress and the appropriate means will be sought.

There are a few other considerations that emerge from the report.

- The federal/provincial 'overlap' in the post-secondary sector is not conducive to optimizing investments in access and quality. Steps must be taken to delineate the respective roles. Building and sustaining capacity to improve access and a post-secondary environment that is competitive with other jurisdictions (states and countries) involves investments in a host of areas – research infrastructure, core infrastructure, undergraduate education, graduate education, international education, sponsored research, student assistance – to mention only a few. Surely there is a way for provincial and federal governments to sort out their respective funding obligations to ensure improved access for students and a quality learning environment that rivals the best in the world.

- Good, consistent, reliable, up-to-date information is a prerequisite to making informed decisions. Efforts must be made to improve the timeliness, quality and breadth of post-secondary information (e.g., enrolment, staffing, financial information) published by provincial and federal governments. In fact a prerequisite to moving towards a more market-oriented approach to funding higher education must necessarily be better information – a legitimate role for government.

Throughout the report reference has been made to the value and necessity of further research in a host of areas as follows:

- the need for better comparative financial and enrolment information with other countries;

- the need for more comparative information about funding mechanisms in other countries;

- the need to catalogue, chronicle and assess the evolving approaches to accountability;

- the link between quality assurance and quality improvement;
- the development of output and outcome quality measures;

- the 'opening up' of the post-secondary system and the impact on competition;

- an evaluation of rankings and licensure requirements, program reviews and various indicators of satisfaction; and

- an examination of the impact of the major increase in research funding on research quality and graduate education.

Clarity of purpose, adequate resources with appropriate funding mechanisms, accountability frameworks focused on results and firmly rooted in institutional governance, recognition of institutional differentiation, more consultation to improve 'trust' among the PSE partners, and better information to inform policy development are the key components necessary to improve access and quality in post-secondary education. Together those components provide an environment where the partnership is strengthened and the probability of success is heightened.

10.1. Concluding Comments

This paper has provided a glimpse at how funding mechanisms and the regulatory environment can affect the ability of post-secondary institutions to address access and quality concerns. It provides some 'food for thought' about the impact of government actions that, hopefully, will help guide the development of better approaches to improving access and quality in the future. There has been a marked change in government attitudes towards post-secondary education over the past few years and improving access and quality are now twin goals that seem to be found in report after report across the country. Moreover, it is now apparent that governments are prepared to increase the 'reinvestment' in post-secondary and improve capacity.

The lessons of the past decade offer a guide for the future.

Appendix A: Funding and Enrolment

As noted in the body of the report there are a number of problems and challenges associated with developing consistent, comparisons of post-secondary financial and enrolment data. While there are Statistics Canada timeseries for both enrolment and financial information, the most recent **actual** data available is 1999 enrolment and 2001 financial information for colleges, and 2003 enrolment and financial information for universities. Given the significant increases in both funding and enrolment over the past few years, in some provinces, it is important to try to factor those changes into the report.

At the same time it is important to recognize that the Statistics Canada enrolment and financial information have a number of limitations in terms of comparability over time. Changes in financial reporting and change in funding practices make historical comparisons less than precise and tend to overstate current income and expenditures relative to earlier years. The evolution of the post-secondary sector has resulted in the introduction of new institutions and new kinds of institutions that have added further complexity to the post-secondary landscape and affected the comparability of historical information. Moreover as noted in the main body of the report there are a number of factors that must be taken into consideration when trying to determine the truly 'discretionary' income available to universities and colleges to meet the on-going costs of core operations.

The main source of the funding trend information is Statistics Canada CANSIM Table 385-0007, University and College Revenue and Expenditures. The information for Table 385-0007 is composed of actual information obtained from Culture, Tourism and the Centre for Education Statistics with Statistics Canada Financial Management System (FMS) *estimates* for more recent years.

The main source of university enrolment is Statistics Canada CANSIM Table 477-0011. Enrolment information for 2004 is based on the Fall 2004 survey of universities by the Association of Universities and Colleges of Canada. Actual college enrolment data to 1999 is from Statistics Canada CANSIM Table 477-0006. Estimates for the period 2000 through 2004 are based on the following:

- in the case of Alberta, British Columbia, and Ontario, annual percentage changes based on other sources of information as detailed in the table;
- in the case of all other provinces except Quebec, the college enrolment increases are assumed to be the same as the university enrolment increases; and
- in the case of Quebec, the college (CEGEP) enrolment has been reduced by 1,000 full-time students per year in recognition of the historical trend and the continued decline in the CEGEP age cohort.[121]

---

[121] Quebec "With regard to enrolment in regular full-time courses at the college level, it is expected that the number of students in pre-university programs will drop by almost 7 percent between Fall 2000 and Fall 2005. After this period, the number of students should grow and, by 2010, return to the level of the late 1990s." *Education Statistics Bulletin*, No. 24 July, 2002, Ministry of Education, Quebec.

The following information is presented to help shed a little more light on the overall funding situation for colleges and universities. There is absolutely no question that college and university revenues have never been higher in absolute terms. The question is: has total revenue – from all sources – kept pace with the overall increase in enrolment and inflation?

Table 1 provides a summary of the total revenue data based on Statistics Canada CANSIM Table 385-0007. The data is indexed to 1992 to facilitate the review **and** adjusted for inflation (CPI) to recognize changes in costs. As noted in the main body of the report the overall increase in absolute dollars is over $11 billion ($27.7- $16.4). Once inflation is taken into account the increase is in the order of $7 billion ($27.7-$20.4) or about 35 percent. However, as noted in the main body of the report, major changes in reporting occurred during the latter part of the 1990s that effectively result in an estimated additional $1 billion in revenue that is solely due to those reporting differences. With the $1 billion removed, the change is reduced to approximately 30 percent.

Table 2 provides college and university full-time enrolments from 1990 to 2004. As noted, actual enrolment figures are only available for colleges to 1999 and for universities to 2003. Estimates have been used to bring the enrolment figures up to date.

Table 3 and Figure 1 provide the result of combining the inflation adjusted total revenue with the full-time enrolment estimates. Essentially funding in six provinces has not kept pace with inflation and enrolment increases, while four provinces are now experiencing total funding levels per student that are higher than 1992-93. However, the calculations must be viewed with caution because:

A) the enrolment data is based on estimates for the most recent years;
B) there have been reporting changes that, on average, would reduce the figures in every province; and
C) the total funding includes funding for **all** purposes (capital, research, operating), regardless of restrictions.

To highlight the latter two points, one only has to look at the Saskatchewan data that is plotted in Figure 1. A major increase in funding occurred in Saskatchewan beginning in 1998 and appears to be a function of significant increases in research funding and changes in financial reporting.

Canada's postsecondary sector would benefit significantly from having more timely and more comparable information to help fully understand the impact funding and enrolment changes over time.

TABLE 1

Total Revenue to Postsecondary Institutions

	1992-93 1993	1993-94 1994	1994-95 1995	1995-96 1996	1996-97 1997	1997-98 1998	1998-99 1999	1999-2000 2000	2000-01 2001	2001-02 2002	2002-03 2003	2003-04 2004	2004-05 2005	% Change
NFLD	$ 324,708	$ 329,645	$ 330,539	$ 337,200	$ 326,201	$ 314,418	$ 320,067	$ 355,295	$ 368,668	$ 384,286	$ 390,390	$ 420,861	$ 427,672	
PEI	72,453	78,930	65,917	80,146	76,132	83,058	85,427	85,427	92,979	100,816	127,965	113,084	118,407	
NS	566,903	496,044	505,766	512,195	513,982	592,008	637,095	727,154	748,754	773,522	830,563	882,420	930,960	
NB	273,278	282,912	288,941	306,244	298,910	306,884	315,383	327,499	342,993	357,923	391,663	392,058	392,060	
Quebec	4,468,317	4,593,187	4,711,311	4,529,608	4,467,677	4,319,658	4,558,645	5,037,556	5,429,763	5,844,014	6,352,027	6,504,598	6,710,042	
Ont	6,018,937	5,936,307	6,031,404	6,422,827	5,823,923	6,121,313	6,545,875	7,613,727	7,924,491	8,371,260	9,109,483	9,295,778	9,909,295	
Man	522,429	516,595	521,841	538,948	545,984	563,421	598,877	658,748	741,365	749,872	822,418	847,088	872,502	
Sask	548,332	551,823	563,141	611,778	632,375	667,235	707,038	737,040	847,599	883,569	947,874	1,006,309	1,043,248	
Alta	1,642,091	1,623,918	1,591,151	1,605,327	1,675,587	1,917,797	2,015,633	2,279,799	2,489,408	2,685,042	2,822,696	2,926,339	3,122,231	
BC	1,932,281	2,010,020	2,149,075	2,272,745	2,325,689	2,455,803	4,233,085	2,509,662	2,695,561	3,056,676	3,464,644	3,642,313	4,070,836	
Total 10	$ 16,369,729	$ 16,419,381	$ 16,759,086	$ 17,217,018	$ 16,686,460	$ 17,341,595	$ 20,015,449	$ 20,331,907	$ 21,681,581	$ 23,206,980	$ 25,259,723	$ 26,030,848	$ 27,597,253	
Canada	$ 16,369,729	$ 16,419,382	$ 16,759,086	$ 17,260,407	$ 16,729,056	$ 17,389,686	$ 20,064,718	$ 20,380,239	$ 21,732,604	$ 23,262,806	$ 25,317,357	$ 26,090,058	$ 27,659,234	69%

Indexed Change

	1993	1994	1995	1996	1997	1998	1999	2000	2001	2002	2003	2004	2005	
NFLD	100	101.5	101.8	103.8	100.5	96.8	98.6	109.4	113.5	118.3	120.2	129.6	131.7	
PEI	100	108.9	91.0	110.6	105.1	114.6	115.6	117.9	128.3	139.1	176.6	156.1	163.4	
NS	100	87.5	89.2	90.3	90.7	104.4	112.4	128.3	132.1	136.4	146.5	155.7	164.2	
NB	100	103.5	105.7	112.1	109.4	112.3	115.4	119.8	125.5	131.0	143.3	143.5	143.5	
Quebec	100	102.8	105.4	101.4	100.0	96.7	102.0	112.7	121.5	130.8	142.2	145.6	150.2	
Ont	100	98.6	100.2	106.7	96.8	101.7	108.8	126.5	131.7	139.1	151.3	154.4	164.6	
Man	100	98.9	99.9	103.2	104.5	107.8	114.6	126.1	141.9	143.5	157.4	162.1	167.0	
Sask	100	100.6	102.7	111.6	115.3	121.7	128.9	134.4	154.6	161.1	172.9	183.5	190.3	
Alta	100	98.9	96.9	97.8	102.0	116.8	122.7	138.8	151.6	163.5	171.9	178.2	190.1	
BC	100	104.0	112.2	117.6	120.4	127.1	219.1	129.9	139.5	158.2	179.3	188.5	210.7	
Total 10	100	100.3	102.4	105.2	101.9	105.9	122.3	124.2	132.4	141.8	154.3	159.0	168.6	

CPI Statcan (1992 = 100)

| | 100 | 101.8 | 102 | 104.2 | 105.9 | 107.6 | 108.6 | 110.5 | 113.5 | 116.4 | 119 | 122.3 | 124.6 | |
| Factor | 1.25 | 1.22 | 1.22 | 1.20 | 1.18 | 1.16 | 1.15 | 1.13 | 1.10 | 1.07 | 1.05 | 1.02 | 1.00 | |

Adjusted for Inflation

	1993	1994	1995	1996	1997	1998	1999	2000	2001	2002	2003	2004	2005	
NFLD	$ 404,586	$ 403,475	$ 403,776	$ 403,216	$ 383,802	$ 364,094	$ 367,222	$ 400,631	$ 404,723	$ 411,358	$ 408,761	$ 428,776	$ 427,672	
PEI	90,276	96,608	80,522	95,837	89,576	96,181	96,090	96,328	102,072	107,918	133,987	115,211	118,407	
NS	706,361	607,142	617,828	612,471	604,742	685,541	730,958	819,940	821,980	828,014	869,648	899,015	930,960	
NB	340,504	346,275	352,961	366,200	351,692	355,369	361,848	369,288	376,537	383,138	410,094	399,431	392,060	
Quebec	5,567,523	5,621,917	5,755,190	5,416,403	5,256,587	5,002,132	5,230,269	5,680,357	5,960,779	6,255,706	6,650,946	6,626,925	6,710,042	
Ont	7,499,596	7,265,853	7,367,774	7,680,271	6,852,321	7,088,435	7,510,270	8,585,252	8,699,485	8,960,988	9,538,165	9,470,596	9,909,295	
Man	650,947	632,296	637,465	644,462	642,395	652,437	687,109	742,805	813,869	802,698	861,120	863,019	872,502	
Sask	683,222	675,414	687,915	731,550	744,041	772,653	811,206	831,088	930,492	945,814	992,480	1,025,234	1,043,248	
Alta	2,046,045	1,987,625	1,943,700	1,919,614	1,971,465	2,220,795	2,312,596	2,570,705	2,732,866	2,874,194	2,955,529	2,981,372	3,122,231	
BC*	2,407,622	2,460,201	2,625,243	2,717,697	2,736,363	2,843,802	4,856,744	2,829,999	2,959,180	3,272,009	3,627,686	3,710,811	4,070,836	
Total 10	$ 20,396,682	$ 20,096,806	$ 20,472,374	$ 20,587,720	$ 19,632,983	$ 20,081,438	$ 22,964,318	$ 22,926,295	$ 23,801,982	$ 24,841,836	$ 26,448,416	$ 26,520,390	$ 27,597,253	35%

Indexed Change

	1993	1994	1995	1996	1997	1998	1999	2000	2001	2002	2003	2004	2005	
NFLD	100	99.7	99.8	99.7	94.9	90.0	90.8	99.0	100.0	101.7	101.0	106.0	105.7	
PEI	100	107.0	89.2	106.2	99.2	106.5	106.4	106.7	113.1	119.5	148.4	127.6	131.2	
NS	100	86.0	87.5	86.7	85.6	97.1	103.5	116.1	116.4	117.2	123.1	127.3	131.8	
NB	100	101.7	103.7	107.5	103.3	104.4	106.3	108.5	110.6	112.5	120.4	117.3	115.1	
Quebec	100	101.0	103.4	97.3	94.4	89.8	93.9	102.0	107.1	112.4	119.5	119.0	120.5	
Ont	100	96.9	98.2	102.4	91.4	94.5	100.1	114.5	116.0	119.5	127.2	126.3	132.1	
Man	100	97.1	97.9	99.0	98.7	100.2	105.6	114.1	125.0	123.3	132.3	132.6	134.0	
Sask	100	98.9	100.7	107.1	108.9	113.1	118.7	121.6	136.2	138.4	145.3	150.1	152.7	
Alta	100	97.1	95.0	93.8	96.4	108.5	113.0	125.6	133.6	140.5	144.5	145.7	152.6	
BC*	100	102.2	109.0	112.9	113.7	118.1	120.0	117.5	122.9	135.9	150.7	154.1	169.1	
Total 10	100	98.5	100.4	100.9	96.3	98.5	112.6	112.4	116.7	121.8	129.7	130.0	135.3	30%

* 1999 index estimated

Adjusted for Inflation and Estimate of Changes in Reporting 130.4

Research Funding

	1992/93		2003-04		2004-05 est.		% Change
Actual	$ 1,709,883		$ 5,049,092		$ 5,800,000		
Estimated	$ 2,130,514 Adjusted for Inflation				$ 5,800,000		172%

Source: CAUBO Financial Statistics of Canadian Universities and Colleges

TABLE 2

University Enrolment
Full-time Graduate and Undergraduate Enrolment

	1990	1991	1992	1993	1994	1995	1996	1997	1998	1999	2000	2001	2002	2003	2004e	% Change 2004 vs. 2003	% Change Since 1990
Canada	532,131	553,955	569,480	574,320	575,715	573,195	573,635	573,100	580,375	593,600	607,255	635,640	675,500	735,600	763,325	3.8%	43.4%
NFLD	12,534	12,912	13,215	13,030	13,145	13,470	13,195	13,165	13,115	14,350	14,400	14,160	14,000	14,400	15,445	7.3%	23.2%
PEI	2,534	2,609	2,725	2,690	2,545	2,425	2,315	2,500	2,470	2,610	2,790	2,785	3,000	3,300	3,485	5.6%	37.5%
NS	27,009	28,601	29,425	29,995	29,920	29,725	29,940	30,075	30,025	29,985	30,895	32,745	33,900	36,200	36,570	1.0%	35.4%
NB	16,895	18,096	19,110	19,495	19,550	19,400	18,930	18,505	18,530	18,230	19,120	19,680	19,900	21,100	21,195	0.5%	25.5%
QUE	124,669	129,993	135,020	137,750	135,605	132,925	132,055	131,075	134,160	137,740	139,410	144,010	153,300	161,800	165,350	2.2%	32.6%
ONT	216,441	225,525	230,570	231,155	230,305	228,160	227,000	227,155	229,985	237,225	242,465	254,190	275,500	313,700	332,210	5.9%	53.5%
MAN	19,698	20,572	20,575	20,295	22,960	21,460	22,025	21,025	20,885	20,865	23,350	24,825	25,200	27,800	28,970	4.2%	47.1%
SASK	21,641	22,393	22,850	23,025	23,180	23,635	23,570	23,865	23,655	23,935	23,875	24,260	25,900	26,500	26,700	0.8%	23.4%
ALTA	48,614	48,791	50,345	51,085	50,805	52,400	53,045	52,825	53,510	55,535	57,995	60,165	62,900	65,000	65,215	0.3%	34.1%
BC*	42,096	44,463	45,650	45,800	47,695	49,595	51,565	53,015	54,040	53,120	52,955	58,815	61,900	65,800	68,185	3.6%	62.0%

*net of University - Colleges

Source: Statistics Canada, CANSIM 477-0011, The Daily, October 11, 2005, and AUCC.

College Enrolment
Full-time

	1990	1991	1992	1993	1994	1995	1996	1997	1998	1999	2000e	2001e	2002e	2003e	2004e	% Change 2004 vs. 2003	% Change Since 1990
Canada	324,529	349,207	364,696	369,192	379,961	391,282	397,308	398,643	403,516	408,781	410,800	415,297	426,425	433,770	439,977	1.4%	35.6%
NFLD	3,666	4,361	4,639	5,000	5,971	5,732	5,704	5,974	5,973	6,576	6,599	6,489	6,416	6,599	7,078	7.3%	93.1%
PEI	999	1,240	923	811	819	996	1,275	1,620	1,899	1,861	1,989	1,986	2,139	2,353	2,485	5.6%	148.7%
NS	2,692	2,653	3,118	3,036	2,765	6,826	6,956	7,307	7,039	7,377	7,601	8,056	8,340	8,906	8,997	1.0%	234.2%
NB	2,664	2,988	3,164	3,248	3,560	3,751	4,808	5,152	5,221	5,366	5,628	5,793	5,858	6,211	6,239	0.5%	134.2%
QUE	154,418	163,768	169,583	169,053	171,997	171,561	166,858	163,550	164,469	162,874	162,000	161,000	160,000	159,000	158,000	-0.6%	2.3%
ONT	99,657	111,362	117,136	121,686	126,433	134,503	141,205	142,353	142,341	143,617	141,946	143,433	150,975	154,523	157,614	2.0%	58.2%
MAN	3,963	4,019	4,067	3,990	3,918	3,612	3,598	3,802	4,181	5,276	5,904	6,277	6,372	7,030	7,325	4.2%	84.8%
SASK	3,433	3,509	3,542	3,593	3,476	3,163	2,787	3,195	2,740	2,918	2,911	2,958	3,158	3,231	3,255	0.8%	-5.2%
ALTA	25,168	25,464	27,291	26,864	27,361	27,928	29,366	29,595	31,999	33,217	35,031	36,448	38,678	40,500	42,800	5.7%	70.1%
BC	27,427	29,288	30,538	31,114	32,800	32,476	34,313	35,599	37,127	39,176	40,665	42,327	43,945	44,862	45,621	1.7%	66.3%
										408,258	410,274	414,765	425,880	433,215	439,414	1.4%	
Year over Year											1.0049	1.0109	1.0268	1.0172	1.0143		

Source: Statistics Canada, CANSIM 477-0006, and estimates beginning in 2000.

Other Sources of College Enrolments

Ontario

	1990	1991	1992	1993	1994	1995	1996	1997	1998	1999	2000e	2001e	2002e	2003e	2004e
FTE	132,689	149,227	158,332	161,576	163,807	168,364	166,080	168,396	169,352	169,001	167,035	168,784	177,659	181,835	
Year over Year											0.988	1.010	1.053	1.024	

Source: Association of Colleges of Applied Arts and Technology of Ontario, Enviromental Scan, 2005

British Columbia

	1990	1991	1992	1993	1994	1995	1996	1997	1998	1999	2000e	2001e	2002e	2003e	2004e
FTE	61,281	63,629	65,925	73,198	74,529	75,405	75,898	76,772	74,035	76,849	79,989	83,048	84,781	86,215	
Year over Year									1.038	1.038	1.041	1.038	1.021	1.017	

Source: Canadian Centre for Policy Alternatives, Financing Higher Learning, Post-secondary Education Funding in BC, November 2004. p.23

Alberta

	1990	1991	1992	1993	1994	1995	1996	1997	1998	1999	2000e	2001e	2002e
FLE								37,489	38,845	40,202	42,397	44,112	46,811
Year over Year											1.055	1.040	1.061

Source: A Learning Alberta: Profile of Alberta's Advanced Education System, June 2005, Supplementary Tables

Total Full-time College and University Enrolment

	1990	1991	1992	1993	1994	1995	1996	1997	1998	1999	2000e	2001e	2002e	2003e	2004e	% Change 2004 vs. 2003	% Change Since 1990
Canada	856,660	903,162	934,176	943,512	955,676	964,477	970,943	971,743	983,891	1,002,381	1,018,055	1,050,937	1,101,925	1,169,370	1,203,302	2.9%	40.5%
NFLD	16,200	17,273	17,854	18,030	19,116	19,202	18,899	19,139	19,088	20,926	20,999	20,649	20,416	20,999	22,523	7.3%	39.0%
PEI	3,533	3,849	3,648	3,501	3,364	3,421	3,590	4,120	4,369	4,471	4,779	4,771	5,139	5,653	5,969	5.6%	69.0%
NS	29,701	31,254	32,543	33,031	32,685	36,551	36,896	37,382	37,064	37,362	38,496	40,801	42,240	45,106	45,567	1.0%	53.4%
NB	19,559	21,084	22,274	22,743	23,110	23,151	23,738	23,657	23,751	23,596	24,748	25,473	25,758	27,311	27,434	0.5%	40.3%
QUE	279,087	293,761	304,603	306,803	307,602	304,486	298,913	294,625	298,629	300,614	301,410	305,010	313,300	320,800	323,350	0.8%	15.9%
ONT	316,098	336,887	347,706	352,841	356,738	362,663	368,205	369,508	372,326	380,842	384,411	397,623	426,475	468,223	489,824	4.6%	55.0%
MAN	23,661	24,591	24,642	24,285	26,878	25,072	25,623	24,827	25,066	26,141	29,254	31,102	31,572	34,830	36,295	4.2%	53.4%
SASK	25,074	25,902	26,392	26,618	26,656	26,798	26,357	27,060	26,395	26,853	26,786	27,218	29,058	29,731	29,955	0.8%	19.5%
ALTA	73,782	74,255	77,636	77,949	78,166	80,328	82,411	82,420	85,509	88,752	93,026	96,613	101,578	105,500	108,015	2.4%	46.4%
BC	69,523	73,751	76,188	76,914	80,495	82,071	85,878	88,614	91,167	92,296	93,620	101,142	105,845	110,662	113,806	2.8%	63.7%
Total 10	856,218	902,607	933,486	942,715	954,810	963,743	970,510	971,352	983,364	1,001,853	1,017,529	1,050,400	1,101,380	1,168,815	1,202,739	2.9%	40.5%

* Canada includes enrolments in the territories

TABLE 3

Total Funding Adjusted for Inflation

	1992	1993	1994	1995	1996	1997	1998	1999	2000	2001	2002	2003	2004e
NFLD	$ 404,586	$ 403,475	$ 403,776	$ 403,216	$ 383,802	$ 364,094	$ 367,222	$ 400,631	$ 404,723	$ 411,358	$ 408,761	$ 428,776	$ 427,672
PEI	$ 90,276	$ 96,608	$ 80,522	$ 95,837	$ 89,576	$ 96,181	$ 96,090	$ 96,328	$ 102,072	$ 107,918	$ 133,987	$ 115,211	$ 118,407
NS	$ 706,361	$ 607,142	$ 617,828	$ 612,471	$ 604,742	$ 685,541	$ 730,958	$ 819,940	$ 821,980	$ 828,014	$ 869,648	$ 899,015	$ 930,960
NB	$ 340,504	$ 346,275	$ 352,961	$ 366,200	$ 351,692	$ 355,369	$ 361,848	$ 369,288	$ 376,537	$ 383,138	$ 410,094	$ 399,431	$ 392,060
Quebec	$ 5,567,523	$ 5,621,917	$ 5,755,190	$ 5,416,403	$ 5,256,587	$ 5,002,132	$ 5,230,269	$ 5,680,357	$ 5,960,779	$ 6,255,706	$ 6,650,946	$ 6,626,925	$ 6,710,042
Ont	$ 7,499,596	$ 7,265,853	$ 7,367,774	$ 7,680,271	$ 6,852,321	$ 7,088,435	$ 7,510,276	$ 8,585,252	$ 8,699,485	$ 8,960,988	$ 9,538,165	$ 9,470,596	$ 9,909,295
Man	$ 650,947	$ 632,296	$ 637,465	$ 644,462	$ 642,395	$ 652,437	$ 687,109	$ 742,805	$ 813,869	$ 802,698	$ 861,120	$ 863,019	$ 872,502
Sask	$ 683,222	$ 675,414	$ 687,915	$ 731,550	$ 744,041	$ 772,653	$ 811,206	$ 831,088	$ 930,492	$ 945,814	$ 992,480	$ 1,025,234	$ 1,043,248
Alta	$ 2,046,045	$ 1,987,625	$ 1,943,700	$ 1,919,614	$ 1,971,465	$ 2,220,795	$ 2,312,596	$ 2,570,705	$ 2,732,866	$ 2,874,194	$ 2,955,529	$ 2,981,372	$ 3,122,231
BC	$ 2,407,622	$ 2,460,201	$ 2,625,243	$ 2,717,697	$ 2,736,363	$ 2,843,802	$ 4,856,744	$ 2,829,899	$ 2,959,180	$ 3,272,009	$ 3,627,686	$ 3,710,811	$ 4,070,836
Total (10)	$ 20,396,682	$ 20,096,806	$ 20,472,374	$ 20,587,720	$ 19,632,983	$ 20,081,438	$ 22,964,318	$ 22,926,295	$ 23,801,982	$ 24,841,836	$ 26,448,416	$ 26,520,390	$ 27,597,253

Total Full-time University and College Enrolment

	1992	1993	1994	1995	1996	1997	1998	1999	2000e	2001e	2002e	2003e	2004e
Canada	934,176	943,512	955,676	964,477	970,943	971,743	983,881	1,002,381	1,018,055	1,050,937	1,101,925	1,169,370	1,203,302
NFLD	17,854	18,030	19,116	19,202	18,899	19,139	19,088	20,926	20,999	20,649	20,416	20,999	22,523
PEI	3,648	3,501	3,364	3,421	3,590	4,120	4,369	4,471	4,779	4,771	5,139	5,653	5,969
NS	32,543	33,031	32,685	36,551	36,896	37,382	37,064	37,362	38,496	40,801	42,240	45,106	45,567
NB	22,274	22,743	23,110	23,151	23,738	23,657	23,751	23,596	24,748	25,473	25,758	27,311	27,434
QUE	304,603	306,803	307,602	304,486	298,913	294,625	298,629	300,614	301,410	305,010	313,300	320,800	323,350
ONT	347,706	352,841	356,738	362,663	368,205	369,508	372,326	380,842	384,411	397,623	426,475	468,223	489,824
MAN	24,642	24,285	26,878	25,072	25,623	24,827	25,066	26,141	29,254	31,102	31,572	34,830	36,295
SASK	26,392	26,618	26,656	26,798	26,357	27,060	26,395	26,853	26,786	27,218	29,058	29,731	29,955
ALTA	77,636	77,949	78,166	80,328	82,411	82,420	85,509	88,752	93,026	96,613	101,578	105,500	108,015
BC	76,188	76,914	80,495	82,071	85,878	88,614	91,167	92,296	93,620	101,142	105,845	110,662	113,806
Total (10)	933,486	942,715	954,810	963,743	970,510	971,352	983,364	1,001,853	1,017,529	1,050,400	1,101,380	1,168,815	1,202,739

Total Revenue (all sources) per Full-time Enrolment

	1992	1993	1994	1995	1996	1997	1998	1999	2000	2001	2002	2003	2004e
NFLD	$ 22,661	$ 22,378	$ 21,122	$ 20,999	$ 20,308	$ 19,024	$ 19,238	$ 19,145	$ 19,274	$ 19,922	$ 20,022	$ 20,419	$ 18,988
PEI	$ 24,747	$ 27,594	$ 23,936	$ 28,014	$ 24,951	$ 23,345	$ 21,994	$ 21,545	$ 21,357	$ 22,621	$ 26,072	$ 20,380	$ 19,836
NS	$ 21,705	$ 18,381	$ 18,902	$ 16,757	$ 16,390	$ 18,339	$ 19,722	$ 21,946	$ 21,352	$ 20,294	$ 20,588	$ 19,931	$ 20,431
NB	$ 15,287	$ 15,226	$ 15,273	$ 15,818	$ 14,816	$ 15,022	$ 15,235	$ 15,650	$ 15,215	$ 15,041	$ 15,921	$ 14,625	$ 14,291
Quebec	$ 18,278	$ 18,324	$ 18,710	$ 17,789	$ 17,586	$ 16,978	$ 17,514	$ 18,896	$ 19,776	$ 20,510	$ 21,229	$ 20,657	$ 20,752
Ont	$ 21,569	$ 20,592	$ 20,653	$ 21,177	$ 18,610	$ 19,183	$ 20,171	$ 22,543	$ 22,631	$ 22,536	$ 22,365	$ 20,227	$ 20,230
Man	$ 26,416	$ 26,036	$ 23,717	$ 25,704	$ 25,071	$ 26,279	$ 27,412	$ 28,415	$ 27,820	$ 25,808	$ 27,275	$ 24,778	$ 24,039
Sask	$ 25,887	$ 25,374	$ 25,807	$ 27,299	$ 28,229	$ 28,553	$ 30,733	$ 30,950	$ 34,738	$ 34,750	$ 34,156	$ 34,484	$ 34,227
Alta	$ 26,354	$ 25,499	$ 24,866	$ 23,897	$ 23,922	$ 26,945	$ 27,045	$ 28,965	$ 29,378	$ 29,750	$ 29,096	$ 28,259	$ 28,906
BC	$ 31,601	$ 31,986	$ 32,614	$ 33,114	$ 31,863	$ 32,092	$ 32,097	$ 30,661	$ 31,608	$ 32,351	$ 34,273	$ 33,533	$ 35,770
Total (10)	$ 21,850	$ 21,318	$ 21,441	$ 21,362	$ 20,230	$ 20,674	$ 23,353	$ 22,884	$ 23,392	$ 23,650	$ 24,014	$ 22,690	$ 22,945

Indexed 1992=100

	1992	1993	1994	1995	1996	1997	1998	1999	2000	2001	2002	2003	2004e
NFLD	100	98.8	93.2	92.7	89.6	83.9	84.9	84.5	85.1	87.9	88.4	90.1	83.8
PEI	100	111.5	96.7	113.2	100.8	94.3	88.9	87.1	86.3	91.4	105.4	82.4	80.2
NS	100	84.7	87.1	77.2	75.5	84.5	90.9	101.1	98.4	93.5	94.9	91.8	94.1
NB	100	99.6	99.9	103.5	96.9	98.3	99.7	102.4	99.5	98.4	104.1	95.7	93.5
Quebec	100	100.3	102.4	97.3	96.2	92.9	95.8	103.4	108.2	112.2	116.1	113.0	113.5
Ont	100	95.5	95.8	98.2	86.3	88.9	93.5	104.5	104.9	104.5	103.7	93.8	93.8
Man	100	98.6	89.8	97.3	94.9	99.5	103.8	107.6	105.3	97.7	103.2	93.8	91.0
Sask	100	98.0	99.7	105.5	109.0	110.3	118.7	119.6	134.2	134.2	131.9	133.2	134.5
Alta	100	96.8	94.4	90.7	90.8	102.2	102.6	109.9	111.5	112.9	110.4	107.2	109.7
BC	100	101.2	103.2	104.8	100.8	101.6	100.0	97.0	100.0	102.4	108.5	106.1	113.2
Total (10)	100	97.6	98.1	97.8	92.6	94.6	106.9	104.7	107.1	108.2	109.9	103.8	105.0

Note the anomaly in British Columbia 1998 data - $ 2 billion increase in revenue of which $1.8 billion was a one-time transfer for capital debt. For purposes of this table the indexed figure and funding per student figure have been held constant for that year.

Figure 1: Indexed Change in Total Funding per Full-time Student (All funds, all sources, adjusted for inflation) 1992=100

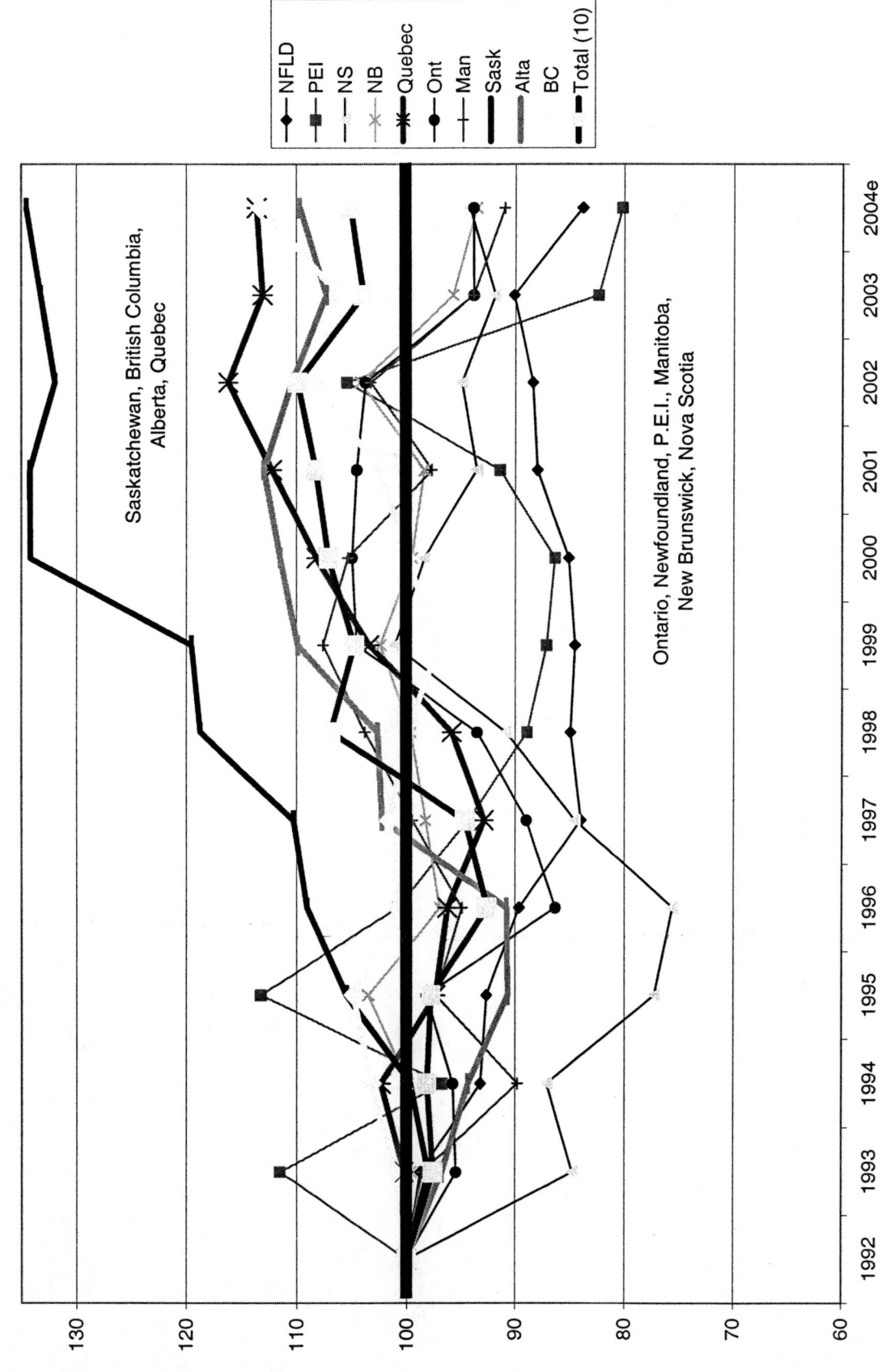

Without a Road Map: Government Funding and Regulation of Canada's Universities and Colleges

Appendix B: Summary of Provincial Allocation Mechanisms and Regulatory Developments

The following summary has been prepared to provide a brief overview of the major allocation mechanisms and key regulatory developments (tuition and degree granting) for each of the provinces. Source documents are cited after each provincial summary. The summary is not intended to be an exhaustive chronology but rather highlight <u>current</u> practice and major changes.[122]

British Columbia	Funding Mechanism	Research	Regulatory
Universities	'Block grant' based on historical allocation. Enrolment targets set for undergraduate and graduate enrolment and gov't targets for specific enrolment areas. Multi-year planning environment, Focus on 'service plans' to delineate funding commitment and accountability	Primarily matching for CFI. Leading Edge Endowment Fund (LEEF) helps fund 20 Chairs – competitive process involving matching fund requirements and limits on the number of applications from individual institutions. Michael Smith Foundation	From 1996/77 to 2001/02, tuition frozen by gov't. Beginning 2002, tuition set by institutions. May 1, 2005 gov't limits tuition increase to 2%. *Access for All* created university-colleges and "applied degrees"
Colleges	Similar to universities. Historical funding set by province. Specific reference to expected enrolment in the 'service plan'	Regional Innovation Chairs (RIC) for colleges and university/colleges	*Degree Authorization Act*. Market opened to 'private' and out-of-province PSE institutions.

J. Malcolmson and M. Lee, *Financing Higher Learning: Post-Secondary Education Funding in BC.*, Canadian Centre for Policy Alternatives, BC. Office, November 2004

J.D. Dennison and H.G. Schuetze, "Extending Access, Choice and the Reign of the Market: Higher Education Reforms in British Columbia, 1989-2004", in *The Canadian Journal of Higher Education*, XXXIV, 3, 2004

D. Fisher, J. Lee, M. MacIvor, J.Meredith and K. Rubenson, *The Development of a Post-Secondary Education System in British Columbia: Transformation and Change*, May 2005

---

[122] For readers interested in a history of funding arrangements in the university sector, in particular, see Peter M. Leslie, *Canadian Universities: 1980 and Beyond*, AUCC, September 1980. For a review of the history of higher education in each province, see Jones, G.A., *Higher Education in Canada: Different systems, different perspectives*, Garland Publishing, 1997.

Alberta	Funding Mechanism	Research	Regulatory
Colleges and Universities	Operating Grant based on historical enrolment-based allocations. Periodic reviews can lead to 'equity' adjustments. Annual inflationary adjustments (if $ available). Targeted envelopes (Access Fund and Performance Fund) New envelopes for Research Excellence and Infrastructure Renewal OTO funding for special situations (i.e., utilities/maintenance) Multi-year business plans	Research Excellence Fund (1996/97) Alberta Heritage Fund for Medical Research Alberta Ingenuity Fund Alberta Science and Research Authority	Provincial Tuition Policy – regulates annual increase AND specifies the tuition 30% of net operating expenditures New tuition policy to be implemented for 2006 Policy for Funding of Private Colleges 1989 – phased to 75% of public grant funding by1998/99 *Post-secondary Learning Act* 2004. The Campus Alberta Quality Council will review proposals from public and private institutions for new degree programs.

Alberta Advanced Education, *A Learning Alberta, Investing in Alberta's Advanced Education System*, June 2005
Report of the MLA Post-secondary Funding Review Committee, 2000

Saskatchewan	Operating	Research	Regulatory
Universities	Weighted enrolment funding formula with targeted envelopes. Formula to be reviewed every 5 years.	**Innovation and Science Fund** (ISF) – supports projects approved by CFI, CRC and Granting Councils	The provincial government appoints half of the members on the universities' Boards of Governors. SIAST, SATCC and the regional colleges are directly accountable to the Minister of Learning for all aspects of the institution or organization. Tuition regulated by province.
Colleges	No funding formula Historical based. Comprehensive review announced in June 2005		

Dr. A. W. Johnson, *Looking at Saskatchewan Universities: Programs, Governance, and Goals* (the "Johnson Report") 1993

The MacKay Report on Universities. 1996 *Report of the Minister's Special Representative on University Revitalization*

Edward DesRosiers and Associates, *Saskatchewan University Funding Review, Final Report*, June 30, 1998.

Manitoba	Operating	Research	Regulatory
Colleges and Universities	Historical based core operating grant - not linked directly to inflation or enrolment. Strategic Envelopes for new programs and restructuring initiatives	**Manitoba Research and Innovation Fund** (MRIF). The MRIF was established to assist in increasing the capabilities of Manitoba universities, colleges, hospitals to compete for federal funds requiring provincial contributions.	The Council on Post-Secondary Education (COPSE) – buffer body Tuition – set at 10% below 1999 level Freeze continues for 2005. Ancillary fees reduced in 2005 via additional grant funding.

The Council on Post-Secondary Education (COPSE) (1996)

Ontario	Operating	Research	Regulatory
Universities	Weighted enrolment funding formula, generates 'base' grant - ~80% of total. No automatic inflation adjustment Use of 'enrolment corridors' Smooths minor enrolment changes. Special purpose envelopes for strategic purposes as defined by government. Special Accessibility funds for major enrolment increases since 2001. Limited Performance Funding	A variety of research initiatives were introduced beginning in 1996 with the Ontario Research Development Challenge Fund (ORDCF) - competitive Ontario Innovation Trust (OIT) –matching federal CFI Premier's Research Excellence Awards Research Performance Fund – 'top-ups' overhead to 40% on provincial research contracts	New Post-secondary Education Quality Assessment Board to review applications to operate private and non-Ontario based PSE institutions in the province. Tuition – regulated by government for majority of enrolment. Some programs are 'cost-recovery'. Regulated programs subject to 2% maximum 2% increase effective 2000/01. Freeze on all tuition imposed for 2004 and 2005. New policy under development.
Colleges	Weighted enrolment – three year rolling average Special purpose envelopes for strategic purposes Limited Performance Funding		

Universities Branch, MTCU, *The Operating Funds Distribution Manual,* various years Research, please see Ontario Budgets 1999, 2000

T. Shanahan, D. Fisher, G. Jones and K. Rubenson , *The Case of Ontario: The Impact of Post-secondary Policy on Ontario's Higher Education System*, draft, May 2005

Quebec	Operating	Research	Regulatory
Universities	Multi-faceted formula. Weighted student funding formula for basic teaching costs. Additional funds for "support for teaching and research" with a separate allocation formula. Separate formula for maintenance of land and buildings. Special purpose envelopes (i.e., graduate funding linked to degrees, library and computer support, ¼ match on donations to maximum $1 million per institution.	Fonds québécois de la recherche sur la société et la culture (FQRSC), the Fonds de la recherche en santé du Québec (FRSQ) and the Fonds québécois de la recherche sur la nature et les technologies (FQRNT) Research Assistance Program to leverage CFI.	Tuition regulated. No tuition increases for Quebec students.
Colleges	CEGEP's set by government		Set by government.

Government of Quebec, *Quebec Policy on University Funding.*
For information on research policies, please see http://www.mdeie.gouv.qc.ca
C. Trottier and J. Bernatchez, *Higher Education Policy in Québec: A Case Study,* draft, May 2005

New Brunwick	Operating	Research	Regulatory
Universities	Unrestricted Operating Assistance represents approximately 95% of total operating assistance to New Brunswick's four public universities, with Restricted Operating Assistance representing the balance The Department of Education is responsible for determining the final allocation of funding. Unrestricted grants allocated as Flat Grant (75% - historical) and Enrolment Grant 25% - based on weighted FTE and three year rolling average.	New Brunswick Innovation Foundation Eligibility for Atlantic Innovation Fund, part of Atlantic Canada Opportunities Agency	Tuition set by institutions, in consultation with government. 2001, Degree Granting Act regulating the delivery process and the quality of degrees offered by private institutions.
Colleges	Restricted purpose grants are small part of overall funding and generally are institution specific or allocated based on share of Operating Grant. Capital funding is project based. No formula. Allocations set by Government.		Set by government.

Correspondence with Maritime Provinces Higher Education Commission

Newfoundland and Labrador	Operating	Research	Regulatory
Memorial University	No provincial funding formula for colleges or the university

Historically based grants set annually by government (moving to 3 year recommendations 2005) | Industrial Research and Innovation Fund – matching CFI allocations

Eligibility for Atlantic Innovation Fund, part of Atlantic Canada Opportunities Agency | Tuition reduced in 2001-02 and recommended freeze for 2005-2007.

Memorial and College of the North Atlantic – closer integration |
| College of the North Atlantic – created effective January 1, 1997 – 5 former regional colleges amalgamated into seven regions with 18 campuses. Governed by a Board appointed by Lt. Governor in Council appointments. | Historically based grants set annually by government. (moving to 3 year recommendations 2005)

Major reductions in funding from 1990/91 through 1997/98 | | *White Paper on Public Post-Secondary Education in Newfoundland and Labrador 2005* recommends

1) 3 joint appointments to MUN and College of North Atlantic Boards

2) 3 Year Performance Contracts |

Government of Newfoundland and Labrador, Report of the Auditor General, *2000 Report Summary booklet*.2000.
Government of Newfoundland and Labrador, *White Paper on Public Post-Secondary Education in Newfoundland and Labrador 2005*

Nova Scotia	Operating	Research	Regulatory
Universities	Weighted enrolment based formula with special purpose grants (location, small size, part-time studies, French language operations) Introduced in 1998.

Some restricted grants for renovations/alteration, library and equipment | The Nova Scotia Research and Innovation Trust works to establish matching funding for provincial research and development projects from national funding programs like the Canada Foundation for Innovation.

Eligibility for Atlantic Innovation Fund, part of Atlantic Canada Opportunities Agency | Nova Scotia Council on Higher Education replaced with Nova Scotia Advisory Board on Colleges and Universities (August, 2000)

Universities currently operating under a *Memorandum of Understanding* regarding grants and tuition fees |
| Colleges
Nova Scotia Community College | No formula. Allocation set by Nova Scotia Government.

"agreed-upon outcomes should serve as inputs to the process of determining the amount of funding which the College should receive. A funding methodology for the Province's contribution to NSCC should be established and roles and responsibilities for the budget process should be clarified."
Auditor General, 1999 | | International fees retained by institution (since late 90s). Grant funding for international students limited to 10% of undergraduate enrolment and 30% of graduate enrolment.

The NSCC Board of Governors recommends tuition levels and the Provincial Cabinet has final approval. |

Government of Nova Scotia, Report of The Auditor General 2000, Chapter 6, Grants to Universities
Government of Nova Scotia, Report of The Auditor General 1999, Chapter 3, Nova Scotia Community College
Nova Scotia Advisory Board on Colleges and Universities, http://nsabcu.ednet.ns.ca/index.shtml

Prince Edward Island	Operating	Research	Regulatory
Universities	Annual grant allocation	Eligibility for Atlantic Innovation Fund, part of Atlantic Canada Opportunities Agency	Tuition regulated by province.
Colleges	Annual grant allocation		

References

Acumen Research. 2005. *Ontario College Applicant Survey 2005, Canada Millennium Scholarship Foundation System Level Report.* Montreal: Canada Millennium Scholarship Foundation.

Astin, A. 1985. *Achieving Educational Excellence: A Critical Assessment of Priorities and Practices in Higher Education.* San Francisco: Jossey-Bass.

Association of Colleges of Applied Arts and Technology of Ontario. 2004. *2004 Environmental Scan.* Toronto: ACAATO

Association of Universities and Colleges of Canada. 2002. *Trends in Higher Education.* Ottawa: AUCC.

Bartleman, The Honourable J.K. 2005 *Strengthening Ontario's Economic Advantage*, Toronto: Government of Ontario.

Bogue, E.G. and R.L. Saunders. 1992 *The Evidence for Quality.* San Francisco: Jossey-Bass.

Barnetson, R.J., and A. Boberg. "Resource Allocation and Public Policy in Alberta's Post-secondary System". *The Canadian Journal of Higher Education.* Vol.30, Issue 2.

Burke, J.C. 2005. *Achieving Accountability in Higher Education.* San Francisco: Jossey-Bass.

Canadian Association of University Business Officers. 2000 *Financial Information of Universities and Colleges, Guidelines, (2000-01).* Ottawa: CAUBO.

Canadian Association of University Business Officers, and Statistics Canada. Various years. *Financial Statistics of Universities and Colleges.* Ottawa: Statistics Canada

Cameron, D. 2000 "Equity and purpose in financing universities: the case of Nova Scotia", in *Canadian Public Administration*, Volume 43, No. 3, Fall.

Cameron, D. 2005. "Post-Secondary Education and Research: Whither Canadian Federalism?" in Iacobucci and Tuohy eds., *Taking Public Universities Seriously.* Toronto: University of Toronto Press,

Challis, J., et.al. 2005 "The University Research Environment", in Iacobucci and Tuohy eds., *Taking Public Universities Seriously.* Toronto: University of Toronto Press.

Committee on University Affairs. 1966. *A Formula for Operating Grants to Provincially-Assisted Universities in Ontario.* Report to the Ontario Ministry of University Affairs, November.

Council of Ministers of Education/Statistics Canada. 2003. *Education Indicators in Canada*, Ottawa: Statistics Canada.

Council of Ontario Universities. 2004. "Ontario Universities – 2004, Resource Document". Toronto: COU. July.

Council of Ontario Universities. 2004. *A History of the Funding Formula in Ontario*. Toronto: COU. (Draft, unpublished, August)

Council of Ontario Universities. 2004. *Proposed University Accountability Framework*, Appendix B. Submitted by COU to the Post-secondary Review, November 15.. Toronto: COU

De Broucker, P. 2005. *Getting There and Staying There: Low-income Students and Post-secondary Education*. Ottawa: Canadian Policy Research Networks.

De Broucker, P., and K. Mortimer. 2005. *Research Summary Table: Access to PSE*. Ottawa: Canadian Policy Research Networks.

Dennison, J. and H. Schuetze. 2004. "Expanding Access, Choice, and the Reign of the Market: Higher Education Reforms in British Columbia, 1989-2004". *The Canadian Journal of Higher Education*. Volume XXXIV, No.3.

Educational Policy Institute. 2004. "The Price of Knowledge, Behind the Headlines", in *epicenter*. Toronto: EPI. Fall.

Edward DesRosiers and Associates. 1998. *Saskatchewan University Funding Review, Final Report*. Saskatoon: Government of Saskatchewan.

Ehrenberg. R. 2005. "Graduate Education, Innovation and Federal Responsibility". in *Communicator*. USA: Council of Graduate Schools. Volume XXXVIII, Number 6, July.

Finnie, R., et al. 2005. "Meeting the Need: A New Architecture for Canada's Student Financial Aid System", in Beach, C.M., et.al., *Higher Education in Canada*. Montreal/Kingston: McGill-Queen's University Press.

Finnie, R. and A. Usher, 2005. *Measuring the Quality of Post-secondary Education: Concepts, Current Practices and a Strategic Plan*. Ottawa: Canadian Policy Research Networks.

Fisher, D, J. Lee, M. MacIvor, J.Meredith and K. Rubenson. 2005. *The Development of a Post-Secondary Education System in British Columbia: Transformation and Change*. Alliance for International Higher Education Policy Studies (AIHEPS). http://www.nyu.edu/iesp/aiheps/

Foot, D.K. 1996. *Boom Bust Echo 2000*. Toronto: Macfarlane, Walter and Ross.

Frenette, M. 2005. *The Impact of Tuition Fees on University Access: Evidence from a Large-Scale Price Deregulation in Professional Programs*. Ottawa: Statistics Canada.

Frenette, M. 2003. *Access to College and University: Does Distance Matter?* Ottawa: Statistics Canada.

George, P. 2005. *Financing Quality in Ontario Universities*, in C.M Beach et.al., *Higher Education in Canada*. Montreal/Kingston: McGill-Queen's University Press.

Gucciardi, F. 2004. *Recognizing Excellence? Canada's Merit Scholarships.* Montreal: Canada Millennium Scholarship Foundation.

Johnstone, D. Bruce. 1998. *The Financing and Management of Higher Education: A Status Report on Worldwide Reforms.* Washington, DC: World Bank.

Jones, G.A. 1997. *Higher Education in Canada: Different systems, different perspectives.* New York: Garland Publishing.

Jones, G.A. 2005. "Complex Intersections: Ontario Universities and Governments", in F. Iacobucci and C. Tuohy, *Taking Public Universities Seriously*. Toronto: University of Toronto Press.

Jones, G.A.. 2004. "Ontario Higher Education Reform, 1995-2003: From Modest Modifications to Policy Reforms", *The Canadian Journal of Higher Education*, Volume XXXIV, No.3.

Jones, G.A., and S.J. Young. 2004. "'Madly Off in all Directions': Higher Education, Marketisation and Canadian Federalism", in Teixeira, P., Jongbloed, B., Dill, D., and Amaral, A., eds. *Markets in Higher Education: Rhetoric or Reality*. Dordrecht, Netherlands: Kluwer Academic Publishers.

Junor, S. and A. Usher. 2004. *The Price of Knowledge 2004: Access and Student Finance in Canada.* Montreal: The Canada Millennium Scholarship Foundation.

Laidler, D., ed. 2002. *Renovating the Ivory Tower: Canadian Universities and the Knowledge Economy.* Toronto: C.D. Howe Institute.

Lang, D.W. 2005. "The Political Economy of Performance Funding", in F. Iacobucci and C. Tuohy, *Taking Public Universities Seriously*. Toronto: University of Toronto Press

Lazar, H.. 2005. *Canadian Fiscal Arrangements: What Works What Might Work Better.* Montreal/Kingston: McGill-Queen's University Press.

Leslie, P.M. 1980. "Canadian Universities, 1980 and Beyond, AUCC Policy Studies No. 3". Ottawa: Association of Universities and Colleges of Canada.

Leyton-Brown, D. 2005. "De-mystifying Quality Assurance", in C.M Beach et.al., *Higher Education in Canada*. Montreal/Kingston: McGill-Queen's University Press.

Mackenzie, H. 2004. *Funding Post-secondary Education in Ontario: Beyond the Path of Least Resistance.* Toronto: Ontario Coalition for Post-secondary Education.

Malcolmson, J. and M. Lee. 2004. *Financing Higher Learning: Post-Secondary Education Funding in BC.* Vancouver: Canadian Centre for Policy Alternatives.

Marshall, D. 2004. "Degree Accreditation in Canada". *The Canadian Journal of Higher Education*, Volume XXXIV, No.2.

Massy, W. 1994. "Measuring Performance: How Colleges and Universities Can Set Meaningful Goals and Be Accountable", in W.Massy and J. Meyerson, eds., *Measuring Institutional Performance in Higher Education.* Princeton, NJ: Peterson's.

Morris C.M., and R. Best. 2005. Notes for a Presentation to the House of Commons Standing Committee on Finance, June 13. Ottawa: Association of Universities and Colleges of Canada.

Pascarella, E. and Terezini, P. 2005. *How College Affects Students:, Volume 2: A Third Decade of Research.* San Francisco: Jossey-Bass.

Riddell, W.C. 2003. "The Role of Government in Post-Secondary Education in Ontario". Background Paper for the Panel on the Role of Government in Ontario.

Schuetze, H. and W. Bruneau. 2004. "Less State, More Market: University Reform in Canada and Abroad". *The Canadian Journal of Higher Education*, Volume XXXIV, No.3.

Shale, D., *Alberta's performance based funding mechanism and Alberta universities.*" Paper presented at the annual conference of the Canadian Institutional Research and Planning Association, 1999.

Shanahan, T., D. Fisher, G. Jones and K. Rubenson. 2005. *The Case of Ontario: The Impact of Post-secondary Policy on Ontario's Higher Education System.* (Draft, May). Alliance for International Higher Education Policy Studies (AIHEPS). http://www.nyu.edu/iesp/aiheps/

Skolnik, M. 2004. "The Relationship of the community college to other providers of post-secondary and adult education in Canada and implications for policy". *Higher Education Perspectives*, Volume 1, No. 1.

Smith, D.C. 2000. *"How will I know if there is quality?"* Report on Quality Indicators and Quality Enhancement in Universities: Issues and Experiences. Toronto: Council of Ontario Universities.

Snowdon, K. 2005. "Assessing the Revenue Framework and Multi-year Planning in the Rae Report", in C.M. Beach, ed., *A Challenge for Higher Education in Ontario.* Montreal/Kingston: John Deutsch Institute for the Study of Economic Policy and McGill-Queen's University Press.

Snowdon, K. 2005. "Muddy Data: University Financing in Canada", in C.M Beach et.al., *Higher Education in Canada.* Montreal/Kingston: McGill-Queen's University Press.

Snowdon, K. 2004. *Applicant Data in Canada: Another Perspective on Access*. Montreal: Canada Millennium Scholarship Foundation.

State Higher Education Executive Officers. 2005. *State Higher Education Finance 2004, Making Sense of Interstate Higher Education Finance Data: Valid Comparisons – More or Less*. Boulder, CO: State Higher Education Executive Officers.

Stein, J.G. 2005. "The Unbearable Lightness of Being: Universities as Performers", in Iacobucci and Tuohy, eds., *Taking Public Universities Seriously*. Toronto: University of Toronto Press.

Task Force on Competitiveness, Productivity and Economic Progress. 2004. *Realizing our prosperity potential*, Third Annual Report. Toronto: Institute for Competitiveness and Prosperity

Trottier C., and J. Bernatchez. 2005. *Higher Education Policy in Québec: A Case Study*. (Draft, May). Alliance for International Higher Education Policy Studies (AIHEPS) http://www.nyu.edu/iesp/aiheps/

Usher, A. 2005. *A Little Knowledge is a Dangerous Thing: How Perceptions of Costs and Benefits Affect Access to Education*. Toronto: Educational Policy Institute.

Wolfe, D. 2005. "Innovation and Research Funding: The Role of Government Support", in Iacobucci and Tuohy eds., Taking *Public Universities Seriously*. Toronto: University of Toronto Press.

Young, S. 2002. "The Use of Market Mechanisms in Higher Education Finance and State Control". *The Canadian Journal of Higher Education*, Vol. XXXII, No.2.

Government Publications

Alberta Advanced Education. 2005. A Learning Alberta, Quality in Alberta's Advanced Education System. June .

Alberta Advanced Education. 2005. A Learning Alberta, Investing in Alberta's Advanced Education System. June.

Alberta Learning. 2000. Report of the MLA Post-secondary Funding Review Committee.

British Columbia. 2005. Ministry of Advanced Education. New Post-Secondary Student Spaces to Date. Ministry website, July 27.

British Columbia2003. Ministry of Advanced Education. An Accountability Framework for British Columbia's Public Post-Secondary Education System.

Newfoundland and Labrador. 2000. *Report of the Auditor General, 2000 Report Summary booklet*.

Newfoundland and Labrador. 2005 *White Paper on Public Post-Secondary Education in Newfoundland and Labrador 2005*.

Nova Scotia. Council on Higher Education. Annual Reports.

Nova Scotia. 1998. Council on Higher Education. University Funding Formula, Technical Report. May.

Nova Scotia. 2000. Report of The Auditor General, Chapter 6, "Grants to Universities".

Nova Scotia. 1999. Report of The Auditor General, Chapter 3, "Nova Scotia Community College"

Nova Scotia. Advisory Board on Colleges and Universities. http://nsabcu.ednet.ns.ca/index.shtml

Ontario. 2005. Ministry of Finance. Ontario Budget, Backgrounder, Reaching Higher: The McGuinty Government Plan for Post-secondary Education. May 11.

Rae, R. 2005. *Ontario A Leader in Learning, Post-secondary Review*. Toronto: Government of Ontario.

Ontario. 2004. Ministry of Training Colleges and Universities, Ontario Universities Branch, *The Ontario Operating Funds Distribution Manual, 2003-04*. December.

Ontario. 2001. Provincial Auditor. Accountability Framework for University Funding: Follow-up (Ministry of Training, Colleges and Universities).

Quebec, Parliamentary Committee on Education for the Quality, Accessibility and Funding of Universities, Consultation Paper.

Quebec. 2002. Ministry of Education. Forecast of Full-time Equivalent Student Enrolment in Quebec Universities, 2001-2002 to 2015-2016, *Education Statistics Bulletin*, No. 24, July.

Quebec. 2000. Ministry of Education. *Quebec Policy on University Funding.*

Saskatchewan. 1996. The MacKay Report on Universities. *Report of the Minister's Special Representative on University Revitalization* Saskatoon: Government of Saskatchewan

Johnson, A.W. 1993. *Looking at Saskatchewan Universities: Programs, Governance, and Goals* (the "Johnson Report") Saskatoon: Government of Saskatchewan

United Kingdom. 2003.. .Department for Education and Skills. *Future of Higher Education*, Executive Summary. http://www.dfes.gov.uk/hegateway/strategy/hestrategy/foreword.shtml.

Universities UK. 2004. *Achieving our Vision.* Spending Review 2004. Submission for England and Northern Ireland. London, England: Universities UK. February.

Our Support

Funding for this series was provided by:
- The Wilson Foundation
- Ontario Ministry of Training, Colleges and Universities
- Power Corporation of Canada
- Fondation Roasters Foundation
- William and Nancy Turner Foundation
- McMaster University
- McGill University
- Queen's University
- University of Alberta
- University of Toronto
- Milton Wong
- First Plazas Inc.

Donations:
BCE Inc.
Power Corporation of Canada
Purpleville Foundation
Scotiabank
SNC-Lavalin Group Inc.

Members of the Board of Directors, Campaign Committee and management team
Many *e-network* subscribers and friends of CPRN

Project Funding:
Corporations:
Bell Canada
Business Development Bank of Canada
CIBC
Ekos Research Associates Inc.
First Plazas Inc.
Home Depot Canada
RBC Financial Group
TD Bank Financial Group

Federal Government Departments,
Agencies and Commissions:
Canada Mortgage and Housing Corporation
Canadian Heritage
Canadian Institutes of Health Research

Citizenship and Immigration Canada
Health Canada
Human Resources Skills Development Canada
Infrastructure Canada
International Development Research Centre
Law Commission of Canada
Office of Nursing Policy
Privy Council Office
Social Development Canada

Provincial Governments:

Alberta
- Alberta Human Resources and Employment

British Columbia
- Ministry of Skills Development and Labour

Manitoba
- Department of Family Services and Housing
- Ministry of Advanced Education and Training
- Ministry of Education, Citizenship and Youth

New Brunswick
- Department of Training and Employment Development

Nova Scotia
- Department of Community Services
- Department of Education
- Department of Environment and Labour

Ontario
- Ministry of Children and Youth Services
- Ministry of Community and Social Services
- Ministry of Labour
- Ministry of Training, Colleges and Universities
- Ministry of Training, Colleges and Universities – Postsecondary Review Secretariat
- Ontario Women's Health Council
- Strategic Planning and Elementary/Secondary Programs

Prince Edward Island
- Department of Education

Quebec
- Commission des normes du travail

Saskatchewan
- Department of Community Resources and Employment
- Ministry of Labour
- Department of Learning

Foundations:
The Bertelsmann Foundation
Bronfman Foundation
Community Foundations of Canada
Walter and Duncan Gordon Foundation
Fondation Roaster's Foundation
Pierre Elliott Trudeau Foundation
William and Nancy Turner Foundation
R. Howard Webster Foundation
The Wilson Foundation

Associations and Other Organizations:
Association of Colleges of Applied Arts and Technology of Ontario
Atlantic Centre of Excellence for Women's Health
Canadian Centre for Philanthropy
Canadian Institute for Health Information
Canadian Labour Congress
Canadian Medical Association
Canadian Public Health Association
Centre of Excellence for Children and Adolescents with Special Needs
Centre of Excellence for Youth Engagement
Conference Board of Canada
McGill University
McMaster University
Modernizing Income Security for Working Age Adults
Organisation for Economic Co-operation and Development
Nuclear Waste Management Organization
Parliamentary Centre of Canada
Public Health Agency of Canada
Queen's University
Social and Enterprise Development Innovations
Task Force Two: A Physician Human Resource Strategy for Canada
University of Alberta
University of Toronto